Celebrating the Earth

Celebrating the Earth

Stories, Experiences, and Activities

NORMA J. LIVO

2000
TEACHER IDEAS PRESS
A Division of
Libraries Unlimited, Inc.
Englewood, Colorado

TEACHER IDEAS PRESS
A Division of
Libraries Unlimited, Inc.
P.O. Box 6633
Englewood, CO 80155-6633
1-800-237-6124
www.lu.com/tip

Library of Congress Cataloging-in-Publication Data

Livo, Norma J., 1929-
    Celebrating the earth : stories, experiences, and activities / Norma J. Livo.
        p. cm.
    Includes bibliographical references.
    ISBN 1-56308-776-6 (paper)
    1. Animals. 2. Animals--Folklore. 3. Animals--Study and teaching--Activity programs.
I. Title.

QL50 .L57 2000
372.3′57--dc21
                                                                      99-059963

This book is dedicated to the naturalists who have come before and led the way.

John Muir

Enos Mills

Rachel Carson

Charles Darwin

John James Audubon

Annie Dillard

George Washington Carver

Luther Burbank

Aldo Leopold

Roger Torrey Peterson

Roger and Laura Sanborn

"Probably the best way to delay death, the best medicine to lengthen life, is to take to the woods. This life sustaining prescription is most effective as a preventative and should be regularly used. Like a sermon, it should be taken once in a while whether needed or not."

Enos Mills (1870–1922)
Father of the Rocky Mountain National Park

Gaelic Blessing

Deep peace of the running wave to you,
deep peace of the flowing air to you,
deep peace of the quiet earth to you.
Deep peace of the shining stars to you,
deep peace of the gentle night to you,
moon and stars pour their healing light on you.

Contents

Stories for Budding Naturalists

Activities for Budding Naturalists

Introduction

Stories and music represent the first ordering of chaos; how else would such seemingly unrelated stories of ptarmigan, bluebirds, snakes, salamanders, goats, bears, skunks, whales, eagles, elk, deer, weasels, and the Perseid meteorite showers be related? That's easy! Consider the Aztec proverb: "The earth will be what its people are." Without a connection to earth and its creatures we live in a world of virtual reality.

My experiences with nature and its spectacular creatures and happenings have created touchstones for my memories. It is often said that what we don't know, we fear. Learning about an animal or plant can only increase our respect for it. Critters that fly, crawl, run, slither, and swim are part of our biological heritage; our appreciation for them now will reinforce our role as responsible stewards for future generations. Scientist Stephen Kellert wrote that we must "start with creatures we can empathize with readily—the larger, charismatic vertebrates— eventually we will need to extend our appreciation to the grandeur found within all living organisms."

We must have firsthand experiences with nature and develop these situations into stories so that we can promote knowledge and respect for these other residents of earth among people around us.

People from the Celts to the Native Americans saw divinity all around them: in the rivers and hills, the sea and sky, in home and village; and within their own souls. Such reverence for the spirit in all things survives to this day.

WHY STORIES?

Through stories we contemplate reality and lessons in life and death. People have used stories to explain how things should be, the way to behave properly, how things and our world came to be. A story's layers of meaning fit the levels of understanding of all listeners and readers. We can return to the same story and discover new things, new ideas, at different stages of our lives.

Stories are light-as-air, deep-as-breath, transforming heirlooms passed down with love, beauty, and form. Everyday stories by and about everyday people can also develop connections for us. Stories promote the understanding of traditional bonds between human beings and the natural world. Stories build awareness.

Stories enchant us. That enchantment reflects the shaman practice of enchanting and entrancing the listener through chants.

Inspiration means a long breath of air; stories make us gasp—ah hah!—as they inspire us. When we retell stories, we keep ourselves alive—they offer us our legacies. Stories give us images of what is worth seeking, worth having, worth doing; they help us dwell in place. Native Americans ground their stories in fields and rivers and mountains and carry their places in mind. Stories help us recognize that we belong to the earth and share this earth with all other creatures; the imaginative bond between person, place, and creature must be nourished.

Folk stories play many roles: they amuse, they instruct, they delight, they catalog collective wisdom; they influence our view of nature and guide us in its mysterious world.

WHY ARE ANIMALS IMPORTANT AS CHARACTERS IN STORIES?

Not because animals are so darn cute; there is much more to it than that. Perhaps animals assume so much importance in folktales because their differences from people make the dramatic events of a folktale or fable a little easier to handle. Animals help us to follow the story while keeping our distance from it; they prevent a frightening story from creating terror in the listener. We often use symbolism to talk about things important to us; the neutrality of animals serves us well. Animals aren't specific, like lazy Uncle John or hysterical Cousin Terry. Animals can masquerade as people dressed in fur, feather, or fin, but as characters they make the story's medicine a little easier to swallow. Stories rehearse the future. Animals as actors ensure smooth rehearsals.

People have credited animals with powers far beyond their own, and ranked them among the earliest of the gods. Some gods assumed the forms of animals when they appeared among men; how else could a mortal explain the snake's shedding of its old skin—wasn't that the stuff of immortality?

Animals also symbolize natural phenomena. Ancient Egyptians saw the sun as a beetle: the beetle lays its eggs in the sand and raps them in a cocoon of manure, which it rolls across the ground just as the sun rolls across the heavens. The legendary phoenix also symbolizes the sun. Doesn't it rise from the tallest trees in the east from the ashes of its former self?

Animals have represented omens and transformed humans. Real and imaginary beasts existed in ancient minds. Could these creatures really have existed and become extinct? Or did ancient people embellish ordinary animals with magic powers? Forms of animals shift and change in stories; language adds confusion in translation. Animals of legend sometimes combine the features of several creatures; often they add human features to their own. Many wear the fabulous mask of invention. These amazing beasts usually possessed supernatural powers and even today maintain an important place in folklore. Writers have given them many names: mythical monsters, exotic zoology, fabulous beasts, and beasts of never.

Animals symbolize human traits: the sly fox, the clever wolf, the powerful bear. Sometimes it helps to see a small, timid animal such as a rabbit outsmart a large, strong animal. After all, aren't we all sometimes helpless in the real world? Wouldn't it be easy for us to relate unconsciously to Br'er Rabbit as he outwits the other animals? Doesn't that give us a sense of power, an "I can do it too" spirit?

MULTIPLE INTELLIGENCE THEORY DEVELOPED BY HOWARD GARDNER

Just who is Howard Gardner and are his theories worthy? Dr. Gardner, a professor at Harvard, an adjunct professor of neurology at the Boston University School of Medicine, and a research psychologist at the Boston Veterans Administration Medical Center, won a MacArthur Prize Fellowship in 1981 to support "Project Zero." He has written extensively on his multiple intelligence theory and his ideas have become guides for current educational strategies. Some of his books include: *The Mind's New Science, To Open Minds, The Unschooled Mind, Multiple Intelligences, Creating Minds,* and *Leading Minds*.

The theory of multiple intelligences presents a way to understand the intellect; it looks at how each of us comprehends, examines, and responds to outside stimuli to solve a problem or anticipate what will come next; this theory shifted the focus from the static measure of "how smart students are" to the dynamic question: "*How* are students smart?" Gardner recognizes background experiences and learning styles as vital elements in students' educational development. "We are all so different largely because we all have different combinations of intelligences. If we recognize this, I think we will have at least a better chance of dealing appropriately with the many problems that we face in the world" (Gardner, *Frames of Mind: The Theory of Multiple Intelligences,* tenth anniversary edition, New York: Basic Books). He believes that intelligences change and develop, that cultural conditions, experiences, and history affect each one of us. Further, he rejects the static concept of inherited versus learned ideas and emphasizes the interaction of environmental and genetic factors.

Once a student of Piaget, Howard Gardner has since reevaluated Piaget's theories of how the human mind works as too narrow. Gardner has developed educational strategies, based on his original seven intellectual capacities, to improve students' learning. Gardner's seven intelligences:

- linguistic
- musical
- logical-mathematical
- spatial
- bodily-kinesthetic
- interpersonal
- intrapersonal

Gardner believes that for students to perform well, they must be challenged; they must believe in themselves and appreciate their individual intelligences.

In 1997, Gardner added an eighth category: naturalist intelligence. According to Tom Hoerr's article "Call of the Wildlife" (*Learning*, September, 1997), a person with naturalist intelligence tends to

- be most comfortable outside;

- be a patient observer of natural phenomena;

- enjoys collecting items such as rocks, leaves, flowers, or shells;

- likes to touch and explore 'yucky things';

- likes to draw, photograph, and record changes in the environment;

- likes to conduct hands-on experiments;

- appreciates detail and notices changes in the environment;

- hypothesizes about relationships between living things;

- sees patterns in the world; and

- nurtures, preserves, and protects the natural world.

What is a naturalist? A naturalist is someone who observes life without idealizing the beautiful or avoiding the ugly. A naturalist advocates or practices the observing of natural history. A naturalist enjoys an innate ability to observe, identify, and classify plants and animals. Gardner describes a naturalist as someone who recognizes flora and fauna and who makes distinctions in the natural world. He further sees a naturalist as someone who uses observation productively: in farming, biological science, hunting, and other nature-related endeavors. Naturalists such as Charles Darwin, Rachel Carson, and John James Audubon, and explorers who wrote and drew about their discoveries have left us new ways to view our world.

Gardner's concept of a naturalist intelligence is important in so many ways to this book, *Celebrating the Earth;* the presence of naturalist intelligence demands that educators present ideas that enchant learners and enhance their powers of observation.

WHAT IS THE PURPOSE OF *CELEBRATING THE EARTH*?

In this book, I have juxtaposed folk stories about nature with my own experiences with nature. Because young learners must recognize the importance of their naturalist skills, these folktales and personal stories provide different ways of observing the same topic.

I have included a section of suggested activities to extend the stories and experiences. *Celebrating the Earth* is a personal statement about the importance of the world around us. Explorers Lewis and Clark discovered a natural world that amazed their contemporaries; my own experiences, too, have sometimes amazed me.

This book also covers intelligences other than naturalist intelligence. Adding the power of story to the topic adds yet another way to examine, observe, identify, and classify our natural world. My goal is to motivate readers to observe and explore their own worlds.

ONE TOUCH OF NATURE MAKES THE WHOLE WORLD KIN

So many people have little knowledge of nature and biology. Park rangers cite numerous odd questions asked them as evidence of the general public's ignorance of the natural world. Such questions as "When do deer change into elk?"; "Is the Grand Canyon man-made?"; "Does Old Faithful erupt at night?"; "How do you turn Old Faithful on?"; and "What time do you feed the bears?" betray a naiveté both humorous and sad.

You, the educator, must protect our children's minds from such blight; through education and a heightened awareness of the natural world, we can destroy these distorted perceptions of natural wonders. I urge you to discover the things that interest youngsters about nature. I urge you to encourage and to cultivate their naturalist intelligence. Our children depend upon you.

Part I

Stories for Budding Naturalists

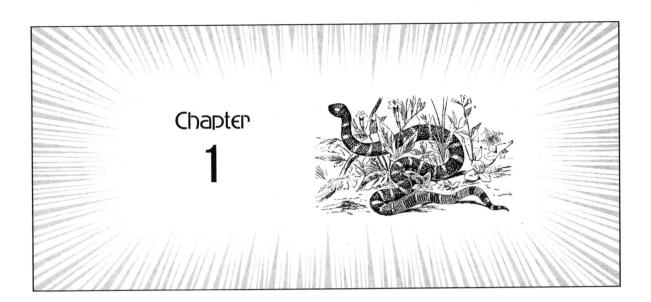

Chapter

1

Amphibians and Reptiles

"Most amphibia are abhorrent because of the cold body, pale color, cartilaginous skeleton, filthy skin, fierce aspect, calculating eye, offensive smell, harsh voice, squalid habitation, and terrible venom; and so their Creator has not exerted his powers (to create) many of them."

Linnaeus, writing in the tenth
Sustema Naturae (1758)

SNAKES

Pumpkin Seed and the Snake
(Hmong)

Once long ago, in another time and place, in a small village, there lived a widow and her two daughters. The older daughter was named Pumpkin Vine and the younger one, Pumpkin Seed.

The family had a garden near the river. They had to work hard to prepare the field for the coming growing season. But they had a problem, because in the middle of the garden was a huge boulder. One day as she was working around the rock, the widow said to herself, "If someone could remove this rock from the middle of my garden I would let him marry one of my daughters."

At the end of the day, the family went home. The next day, the three women went back to work in the garden and found that the rock was gone! The widow started to laugh and said out loud, "I was only joking. I wouldn't allow either of my daughters to marry whoever removed that rock."

The widow thought that was the last of the giant rock. But the very next day, when the widow and her daughters went back to the field to work, there was the rock, in its original place in the middle of the garden.

Once more the widow said to herself, "If someone would take this rock from the middle of the field I would let him marry one of my daughters."

The next day the rock was gone again, but the widow said, "I did not mean it. I wouldn't allow either of my daughters to marry whoever removed that big rock," and she laughed.

The next morning the rock was back in its spot, and the widow again promised one of her daughters in marriage to the person who could remove the rock.

Just like the other times, the rock disappeared from the field and the widow again teased, "I did not mean it. I wouldn't allow either of my daughters to marry the person who moved the big, heavy rock."

The next morning the widow went to the field alone and found the rock back in its place. Giggling a little, the widow whispered, "If someone would take this rock from the middle of the field I would let him marry one of my daughters."

This time, a snake that was nearby said, "If you promise not to lie anymore I will remove the rock."

The widow was so startled that she promised not to lie anymore. The snake slithered from the edge of the garden, placed his tail around the rock, and threw it into the river. Since the widow's two daughters hadn't come to the field with her, the snake followed the widow home.

When they got home the widow called from outside to her daughters. She told them what had happened and said that one of them would have to marry the snake. Neither Pumpkin Vine nor Pumpkin Seed wanted to marry the snake. They refused to open the door and let the snake into the house.

The snake and the widow waited and waited until it was dark, but the girls wouldn't open the door. Then the mother whispered through the door to her daughters, "I will kill the snake when he falls asleep." Even though her mother had said this would work, Pumpkin Vine, being the older one, still refused to open the door. It was very dark outside by this time. Pumpkin Seed, on the other hand, thought that things would go as easily as her mother said, so she opened the door.

When the snake got into the house, Pumpkin Vine and Pumpkin Seed were frightened by its huge size and shininess. Pumpkin Vine protested bitterly when her mother asked her to marry the snake. The widow finally convinced Pumpkin Seed to marry the snake. The snake followed Pumpkin Seed wherever she went. It curled up beside her feet when she sat down. When she went to bed, the snake slid into her bed and coiled up beside her.

That night, with a sharp knife in one hand and a candle in the other, the widow crept into Pumpkin Seed's bedroom to kill the snake. But she discovered it was not an ugly snake sleeping beside Pumpkin Seed, but the most handsome young man that she had ever seen. She couldn't kill him.

The next day when Pumpkin Seed woke up the snake was still alive. She cried and demanded to know why her mother hadn't kept her promise to kill it. "I'll kill the snake tonight, Pumpkin Seed. Please trust me," begged the widow.

That night, the snake again slid into Pumpkin Seed's bed and coiled up beside her. The widow came into the room with her sharp knife and the candle and crept up to the bed to kill the snake. Again, though, instead of an ugly snake sleeping beside Pumpkin Seed, it was the handsome young man. Once more, she just couldn't kill him.

The next morning Pumpkin Seed woke up and there the snake was in her bed, still alive. She cried and cried and demanded to know why her mother hadn't killed it. "I'll kill the snake tonight, Pumpkin Seed. Please give me one more chance. Please trust me," pleaded the widow.

When the sun rose the next morning bright and warm, Pumpkin Seed woke up and there was the snake—still alive. Now Pumpkin Seed had no choice. She had to go with the snake to his home and be his wife. On the way they came to a lovely clear stream. "Pumpkin Seed, I will go take a bath over behind the rocks. You wait here while I am gone."

"All right," Pumpkin Seed agreed.

"When I am gone, you will see lots of colorful bubbles pouring down the stream. You must not touch the green bubbles. You can play with the white and yellow ones, but do not touch the green bubbles," warned the snake. Pumpkin Seed nodded in agreement.

The snake had been gone for a while when, sure enough, Pumpkin Seed noticed a variety of colored bubbles floating down the stream. She stood in delighted amazement as the bright, glittering bubbles traveled smoothly with the clear water. She eagerly captured some of the yellow bubbles. To her surprise the bubbles turned into gold jewels in her hands. Then she gathered some white bubbles, and they turned into silver jewels. Pumpkin Seed was quite pleased. She had never seen such beautiful riches. She gaily put them on her neck, her wrists, her ears, and all her fingers.

As she was admiring them she thought, "Why shouldn't I have some of the green bubbles?" So she reached down and scooped up some green bubbles, and before her startled eyes they turned into twisting snakes in her hands. They even stuck all over her hands. She frantically tried to remove the snakes, but they wouldn't come off.

A moment later, a young handsome man came toward her and she quickly hid her wriggling snake-covered hands behind her back. "Why are you hiding your hands?" asked the man.

Her voice quivered as she told him, "Oh, my husband is a snake. He went up the stream to bathe and he told me to keep my hands like this."

The young man smiled and said, "I am your husband . . ."

Pumpkin Seed interrupted him. "No, you can't be!"

The man smiled and said, "Look at this! He raised his arm and showed her the remaining snakeskin in his armpit. She believed him when she saw the skin and felt ashamed when she showed him her hands.

To her surprise, he simply blew on her hands and the snakes fell off and disappeared like magic. They went home and lived happily for the rest of their lives.

Adapted from *Folk Stories of the Hmong* by Norma J. Livo and Dia Cha (Englewood, Colo.: Libraries Unlimited, 1991), 79–82

About the Story

This story is about magic. Not only is it full of magic, it is full of folklore. The Yokut shamans of central California lure snakes from their dens in early spring and use them in curing ceremonies; the Hopi present snake dances as a prayer for rain. In ancient Egypt and many cultures of the past, the phallic-shaped serpent symbolized fertility and creativity. In Asian cultures, the snake controls moisture and symbolizes power.

Personal Story

My personal snake story goes back to our family farm in western Pennsylvania. Black snakes were the farmer's joy because they kept the barns free of rodents as well as dangerous copperheads. Because black snakes were valued and protected, we were raised with a positive view of them.

On one of the first warm spring days in March, we were all up at the farm and decided to go for a hike over the fields into the woods to visit a giant oak tree. My husband, George, and I, our four children, and my father went on this glorious trip. Our daughter, Lauren, was at that time in the throes of practicing baton twirling because she planned to try out for the high school majorettes. As we picked our way through the stubble of last year's crops and walked almost single file, Dad was teasing Lauren and laughing at her as she walked in front of him twirling the ubiquitous baton.

We reached the edge of the woods and were about to cross a little ravine where the stream was flowing when something made me look up instead of at my feet. The trees were still without leaves but their branches looked unusual: They were fat; they were . . . *moving!* Black snakes of all sizes curled on every branch and twig. They dripped from the trees like black icicles.

I called out to the gang to look. We all stood in awed silence as we watched the aerial dance of the snakes in the trees. They were doing just what we were all doing—enjoying the sun on this first spring-like day. The kids stood quietly and full of amazement; never had they seen that many snakes in one place before.

But Dad's reaction completed the magic of it all. There he was, a grandfather, raised on that farm, and he had never seen such a sight, either. He was speechless. We all rejoiced in the gift of witnessing this spring ritual.

When we returned from our walk that day, Lauren forgot to twirl her baton. Later, we all compared notes on what we had seen. The kids tried to give estimates as to how many snakes we had seen gathering, but my most vivid impression remains the great pleasure Dad experienced from this "first."

We hiked in that area in other years, but never again did we see our sunbathing snakes. Ah, but magic lingered in the possibility that we might. Now that I am a grandmother, I realize how rarely we experience "firsts"—and even "seconds."

SALAMANDERS

The Salamander of Fire
(Aristotle and Pliny)

The five-year-old Benvenuto Cellini, an Italian artist of the sixteenth century was in a room where a good fire of oak was burning. Looking into the flames he saw a little creature that looked like a lizard, in the hottest part of the fire. His father told him it was a salamander and an amazing creature. Aristotle saw an animal in the center of a blazing fire. According to Aristotle, "That creature not only resists fire, but extinguishes it. When the salamander sees the flame he charges it as an enemy which he knows how to vanquish." (See Figure 1.1.)

One winter in ancient times, a tribe member hauled a hollow tree to the fireplace for fuel to keep himself warm. As he sat there gazing into the embers of the fire, he threw the hollow tree into the fire. The fire flared. A bright flame danced up and in the middle of the sparking flames the tribesman saw a salamander put forth all its magic to defend itself from the fire.

Figure 1.1   Salamander "lives from fire and extinguishes it." J. Boschius, 1702.

In the 1980s, the men from a drilling team lit a kerosene heater to warm their hands as they worked with the cold steel used in drilling. As has happened so often, from the bottom of the heater, called a salamander, raced a real salamander.

In none of these events over the ages was anyone able to capture one of these magical creatures.

The salamander has been called the fire of passion, the fire of wisdom, and the fire of virtue. It is the salamander of fire.

About the Story

A magic salamander appears in Jewish tradition, the phoenix and the salamander feature in Arabian and Persian cultures, and in the Middle Ages, salamanders decorated the bestiaries.

Although the salamander superficially resembles a lizard, it is a scaleless amphibian covered with a soft moist skin and breathes with gills in the larval stage. It inhabits moist, mossy woods, particularly peat moss. The salamander breeds in peat bogs and mossy areas bordering streams. Females lay eggs deep between the moss plants; the larvae live in the water for a short while before migrating onto land.

Ancients believed the salamander not only resisted fire, but extinguished it by charging the flames to vanquish them. The salamander's skin resists fire; the salamander secretes a milky juice from his pores when he is irritated. This secretion defends the body from fire for a few moments. A story tells of a salamander (captured as it escaped from a fire) suffering bad burns on its feet and parts of its body.

In winter, the salamander hibernates in hollow trees or other cavities, where it coils itself and lives in a torpid state until spring.

During the Renaissance, salamanders became *vulcanales* and their offspring *tinder*. The Sicilians called the salamander a "bird colder than any other," and believed that it lived in Mount Etna, Sicily's active volcano.

Salamanders symbolize the ability to maintain focus and integrity, even in times of confusion and adversity. When salamanders lose their tails or legs through injury, they grow new ones; scientists have discovered that the injured flesh creates small electric currents that stimulate the growth of new cells. Although human beings cannot replace a lost finger, our bodies do heal cuts and mend broken bones. Researchers have found that when they send a tiny electric current through a broken bone, the break will heal in about half the normal time.

Personal Story

Our western Pennsylvania home perched on a heavily wooded hillside and was a perfect place to ride sleds. As a kid I used to go up on the very hill that my husband and I later owned and sled down it. The day I hit a tree, I learned how to steer to avoid bodily damage. I remember those rides vividly.

We bought the house and the lots beside it in 1957; our four children played all over the hillside with their friends. The springs at the top of the hill made the perfect "mucking around" place for kids to dig, dam, build, and mess around.

One spring day, as I was washing dishes, I heard bloodcurdling screams coming from the top of the hill. From the intensity of the screams, I knew this was an emergency; I ran out of the house and started up the hill.

Our six-year-old daughter, Lauren, leapt down the hill clutching her wrist—still screaming. As I ran, I planned how I would get her to the hospital to have her hand reattached; I was certain that she had severed her hand from her arm. When I reached Lauren, there was no blood. She held her hand out to me with a joyous scream: salamander eggs clustered on her palm—*hatching!*

At that moment, a herpetologist also hatched. Today, Lauren is a professional herpetologist who just completed her doctorate and, with the Colorado Division of Wildlife, conducts research on boreal toads. She is a professional photographer (specializing in, as she says, "herps"), and has written a book and numerous articles on her beloved critters.

Not many people can point to the exact moment a young person received the "calling" for a professional and personal life. Yes, salamanders symbolize the ability to maintain focus and integrity even in times of confusion and adversity! I was there to see (and hear) it.

Chapter 2

Flying Creatures

"Attentive listening is a skill that takes some practice. When people lived close to nature, listening to the world around them was essential— for finding food, for defense and just to keep tabs on what was going on around them. We have trained ourselves to tune out much of the sounds around us. We must remember to listen."

Mary Taylor Young

BIRDS

The Bluebird and the Coyote
(Pima)

Once there was a lake where no river flowed in or out. The water in this lake was a clear blue—indeed, the lake was so clear you could see the pebbles and rocks glistening deep at the bottom. One of the lake's regular visitors was a bluebird. This wasn't a bluebird as we know it today; it was a very ugly-colored bird. Each morning for four mornings, the bird bathed in the lake four times. Each morning as it bathed, the bluebird sang:

> *There's a blue water,*
>
> *It lies there,*
>
> *In I went each morning,*
>
> *And now amazing and true,*
>
> *I too am all blue.*

On the fourth morning after its fourth bath, the bird lost all its feathers and came out of the lake in its bare skin—not really a very pleasant sight. However, on the fifth morning, the bird looked quite different—all its new feathers were blue. The bird was clothed in a bright blue like the blue of the sky overhead; like the blue of the lake where no river flowed in or out and where you could see the pebbles and stones glistening far down on the bottom.

While all this was happening, Coyote had been observing the bird as it bathed. When he saw how brilliantly blue the bird was now, Coyote wanted to jump in and get his fur changed because he didn't like its bright green color. There was just one big problem! Coyote was afraid of water—in fact, he hated water!

On that fifth morning, when the bird was blue, blue, blue, Coyote said to Bluebird, "How has it happened that all your ugly color has gone and now you are blue, beautiful, and so happy? You are more beautiful than anything that flies in the air, more beautiful than all the other birds. You are the most beautiful creature I have ever seen. I would like to be blue like that. I would like the other animals to see me and admire how blue and beautiful Coyote can be."

Coyote thought that his being bright blue would make him beautiful and the envy of all the other animals. "I bathed four times for four mornings in the blue lake," said the Bluebird. Bluebird was so pleased that Coyote thought him beautiful that he even taught Coyote the song:

There's a blue water,
It lies there,
In I went each morning,
And now amazing and true,
I too am all blue.

Coyote, in spite of his fear and hatred of water, cautiously went into the lake the next morning to bathe. The second morning, he again bathed and the water felt cool. On the third morning, he almost enjoyed the feel of the water. The fourth morning, the lake was soothing and delightful. Sure enough, on the fifth morning, Coyote was as blue as little Bluebird.

Coyote felt so proud as he looked at his feet, legs, and, best of all, his tail. He was beautiful! He looked around to see if anyone was noticing how beautiful and blue he was. He strutted around the lake hoping other creatures would see him. Coyote even decided to check on his shadow to see if it was blue, too. Because he wasn't watching where he was going, he bumped with a thump into a stump. He landed in the dirt on the road and because his fur wasn't completely dry yet, he became dust-colored all over. That is why, to this day, coyotes are the color of dust.

About the Story

In the open meadows of the high country, nothing is more beautiful than a blizzard of bluebirds; it is like a flash of summer sky. To many seasoned Colorado bird-watchers, the return of the bluebird to the prairies and mountains heralds springtime in the Rockies (see Figure 2.1, page 14).

All three species of North American bluebirds make their home in Colorado: the western bluebird, the mountain bluebird, and the eastern bluebird. The mountain bluebird lives in open grasslands and sage shrub lands adjacent to open aspen, and pine-forested habitat as high as 13,500 feet.

Appropriate housing is unquestionably the major problem facing the reproductive success of bluebirds throughout the country. The destruction of old or standing dead trees and the replacement of old, rotting wooden fence posts with treated and steel posts has created the housing shortage for the bluebird.

Personal Story

So that he can study, trace, and encourage the growth of bluebird populations, Dr. Robert Cohen, a retired science professor, has received grants to build birdhouses and place them in some of these mountain meadows. He has built hundreds of birdhouses, which he has attached to fence posts. When the young birds hatch, he bands them so that he can follow their progress accurately.

George (my husband) and I have seen the bluebirds in these areas and can attest to the success of Dr. Cohen's houses and efforts. We are always joyful to discover another meadow filled with bluebird houses and their occupants.

Figure 2.1   Bluebirds staging at Rocky Mountain National Park, September 1999.

Labor Day had come and gone and the following week, George and I made a trip to the mountains just to poke around. Summer vacationers had left and we had the roads and sights to ourselves. This is the wonderful time of year to poke around because the roads are not clogged with campers and recreational vehicles as they struggle up the steep grades and slow the traffic.

We spent that day taking every side road we came to and discovered many pleasant locations. We sat on the shores of lovely mountain streams and lakes and felt healed and at peace. Our greatest surprise came when we drove our Jeep into a now-deserted campground to have a picnic lunch. At the entrance we flushed hundreds of bluebirds—a blizzard of bluebirds! Never had we seen so many bluebirds collected in one place. It was one of the most exciting nature observations we had ever made.

Several weeks later, on another of those special fall days in the mountains, we came upon Dr. Cohen as he made his rounds of the birdhouses, cleaning them out and getting them ready for the next nesting season. We pulled off the road to talk to him and watch him as he worked. During the conversation we told him about our sighting at the campgrounds. I saw our conversation as one of those great moments of irony: here was a sincere, dedicated scientist, who cherished as one of his goals the building up of the bluebird population, talking with a couple of sincere but amateur nature lovers who had told him something they thought he might be interested in.

Interested? Tears glistened in his eyes as we told him about the gathering of the bluebirds in the campground. He told us that we had witnessed a "staging." A staging happens when the bluebirds gather and prepare for their migration south. We had stumbled into this amazing happening; Dr. Cohen, who had spent much of his life working to perpetuate this species, had *never* seen a bluebird staging. He took out a small spiral notebook and jotted notes about where we had seen the birds and when, and continued his work. I thought his shoulders drooped a bit as we said our farewells.

That evening, as we sat watching the sun set on a hillside overlooking a lake that reflected the last of the blue fall sky, we heard coyotes howling. Could this have been the lake where the bluebird took his baths and changed from an ugly-looking bird to one of great beauty and worthy of the work, study, and dedication of a scientist who had loved bluebirds since his childhood?

Ptarmigan

(Japan)

A long time ago when monsters and giants still lived in the mountains of Japan, a group of hunters came upon some ptarmigan, the "thunder bird," which is sacred to the thunder god. That same night, all but one of the hunters mysteriously disappeared. The young hunter who was left went to search for the others.

He found them in the home of Snow Woman, who slaughters everyone who strays into her domain in the high mountains. Her house was made of smooth rocks from the fields around, which were covered with lichen. Moss was stuffed between the rocks. The young hunter saw a picture of a ptarmigan hanging in the doorway. He knew that it was there to keep the lightning away.

The young hunter called to Snow Woman just as she whacked the last of the lost hunters over his head. "Why do you kill all who stray into your territory?" he demanded.

Snow Woman turned to seize him but was struck by something special about this man. "I kill those who come here and stay too long because they threaten me and the mountains," she replied. As Snow Woman and the hunter talked, she grew gentler and came to care about this brave, earnest young man.

She decided not to kill him as she had always done with others. "You must go now," she told him. "You have stayed too long in the mountains. I will spare your life but only if you promise not to tell anyone about me and what you have seen here. If you tell anyone, I will slay you."

The young hunter made the promise and left her home and the mountains. As he passed through the doorway of Snow Woman's home, he noticed that the eyes of the ptarmigan in the picture appeared to watch him. He climbed down the mountains. Because he was above tree line, there were only rocks in the fields where he walked; but as he looked closer, one of the rocks moved. The moving rock was a camouflaged ptarmigan, who blended right into the surroundings. The ptarmigan in his mottled colors showed no fear of the hunter.

Years went by and the young man told no one of his adventures while hunting in the mountains, but friends noticed that he was somehow different. He seemed detached. Everyone was pleased for him when he met a beautiful young raven-haired maiden at a local festival and fell immediately in love with her.

The raven-haired maiden returned his love and so they married. She hung a picture of a ptarmigan in the doorway of their home to protect them from lightning. Happy years passed and they were blessed with beautiful children that looked like their mother.

One beautiful moonlit evening as they sat in their cozy kitchen and talked, the moonlight lit up the ptarmigan picture; the picture reminded the husband of the Snow Woman and how she had spared his life. He felt secure and safe with the woman he loved. "I want to share a very important time of my life with you," he said. He told her of the hunting trip, the mysterious disappearance of his hunting friends, and how he had found them all killed by the Snow Woman of the mountains. "The ptarmigan picture in the moonlight reminded me of that time. I'll never know why she spared my life."

His wife looked at him with a dreadful sadness. "You have broken the promise you made to the Snow Woman never to tell anyone about her," she said with a hoarse whisper. "And now it is done! I am the Snow Woman. Even today I cannot kill you but with great sadness for all I leave behind, I must now leave you and go back to the mountains."

Before his startled eyes, his beautiful raven-haired wife, the mother of his children, turned into Snow Woman. As Snow Woman left their home, the husband heard her wailing as she disappeared into the shimmering moonlight.

For the rest of his life he was constantly reminded of what he had lost when he looked at his children or at the picture of the ptarmigan.

About the Story

Ptarmigan (see Figure 2.2) live in the mountains, near timberline, from Mexico to Alaska. They are like chameleons in the way they blend into their surroundings. In winter, ptarmigan turn white; thus their name "moving snowballs." In spring, their soft feathers change to a mottled brown and white, again giving them excellent protection. They move slowly, barely detectable among the rocks and patches of snow.

The ptarmigan, about 12 inches long, belongs to the grouse family. When other birds migrate south for the winter, the ptarmigan flies above the tree line where the cold winter winds blow the snow from the ground and reveal the winter food supply. In the spring, the ptarmigan travels from the mountain tops to feast on the new growth of dwarf willow in the valleys.

The ptarmigan will actually burrow into a snow bank to spend the night. Because dense feathers cover its shank and foot, the ptarmigan possesses a natural snowshoe with four times the walking surface of a bird having an unfeathered foot. The ptarmigan's scientific name is *lagopus leucurus; lagopus* is Greek for "harefooted." The soft feathers of the ptarmigan were once used as stuffing for bedding.

Figure 2.2   Ptarmigan. Photo by Norma Livo.

Personal Story

My oldest son, Eric, invited me to join him on a trip to the mountains. He headed for Mosquito Pass between Leadville and Fairplay, in Colorado. It was a bright summer day and we had the mountains to ourselves. When we started to climb the pass, we found the road in rough condition, so Eric stopped to put the truck into four-wheel drive. We continued up the steep road and the truck (to my thinking) was leaning rather frighteningly with the driver's side at a steeper pitch than the passenger's side (my side). Because the tilt left me feeling insecure, I asked Eric to stop and let me off. "I'll meet you at the top of the pass," I said. "With me out, the truck might not lean so much."

Eric scoffed at me, but I insisted. He stopped and I got out. He slowly took off again on his climb upward; the truck kicked up loose rocks and stones from the trail.

I hadn't taken a dozen steps before I saw a "moving rock." I looked closer and there I saw two of them: my first ptarmigan! What a thrill for me. I quickly got my camera out and started clicking away. I noted the mottled brown and white feathers and the red line that appeared just above the birds' eyes.

The ptarmigan moved slowly and didn't seem to fear me, so we continued our rambling around the rocks and boulders. I shot 36 slides of this wonderful moment.

When I finally reached the top of the pass, I found Eric and the truck safely there. Eric was admiring the view when I puffed up, wildly bragging about what I had almost literally stepped on when I got out of the truck.

I will always think of Mosquito Pass as "Ptarmigan Pass." Every time I look at my 36 photographs (and they did turn out with fantastic clarity), I live that wonderful experience again.

A Bird Couple's Vow
(Hmong)

Many, many New Year's festivals ago, a pair of birds vowed to love each other for life and to never leave each other. When they needed to build a nest, they ended up laying their eggs on the beard of a spirit man. One evening, the male bird flew off to find food. He landed on a lotus flower and sucked the nectar from the flower for quite a while. But suddenly the sky became dark and the flower closed up, whoomp, with the bird inside. He couldn't get back to the nest that evening and had to spend the night inside the flower. When the male bird didn't return, the female bird thought that her husband had left her.

In the morning, when the sun came up and shone on the flower, the flower opened and the bird was able to fly back home. When he got there, his wife said to him, "Why were you out so long? Were you out talking with other girls?"

"No," said the male bird. "I didn't talk to anyone. I went to suck nectar from a water lily and, while I was sucking, it closed up and I couldn't get out."

The female bird didn't believe him. Being very clever, the male bird said, "I swear this is true. If it isn't true, may something bad happen to the spirit man." When the spirit man heard that, he was quite angry, so he cut off the nest from his beard and threw it away in a valley of long, tall grass, the kind that was used to make thatch for roofing.

Shortly after, the eggs hatched. One day, the village people came to the valley to burn the grass where the birds were living. As the fire burned closer and closer, the female bird said to her husband, "Let me stay on top of the chicks and you stay on the bottom. Let both of us die with our chicks."

The male said, "No. Let me stay on top and you stay on the bottom." Finally, the female let the male stay on the top. The fire raged up to their nest and burned it, but the male flew away, letting his wife die with the chicks. The female died, but she remembered that her husband had left her to die in the nest with their little chicks.

The female bird was reincarnated as a king's youngest daughter. She remembered her life as a bird, and she couldn't forget the things that her bird husband had done. They made her so angry that she couldn't speak.

After the male bird had flown away from his wife and chicks, he also died; he was reincarnated as a working man.

One day the king proclaimed, "If anyone can make my daughter talk, I will let her marry that person."

Shortly after that, a young man heard about the king's promise. He went to Shoa (which means wise prophet in Hmong) and said, "Shoa, I want to marry the king's daughter. Please help me and tell me what I can say to this lady that would make her talk to me."

Shoa remembered the birds and said, "Don't you remember when fire burned the valley of the long, tall grass? You flew away and let the female bird die with your chicks. You only need go to her and tell her what you did. But instead of saying that you flew away and left her and the chicks to die, you should say that the female flew away and the male died with the chicks. Then she will answer you, of course."

So the young man traveled to the king's palace. He said to the king's daughter, "Let me tell you a story. A long time ago, there were a couple of birds. They made a nest on the spirit man's beard. But the spirit man cut off their nest and threw it into the valley of the long, tall grass. When people burned the valley of grass, the male bird said that he should stay on top of the chicks and that both he and his wife would die with the chicks in the fire. The female disagreed, so the male let the female stay on top of the chicks and he stayed under them. But when the fire burned their nest, the female flew away and left the male to die with the chicks."

The girl spluttered and cried, "You are wrong! The male bird was on top!" The man answered, "No, the female was on top."

They kept arguing back and forth about which bird was on the top. The king heard them and said, "This young man has succeeded in getting my daughter to talk. I will keep my promise and let him marry her."

So they were married, and that is how the couple once again became husband and wife.

Adapted from *Folk Stories of the Hmong* by Norma J. Livo and Dia Cha (Englewood, Colo.: Libraries Unlimited, 1991), 64–66.

About the Story

As is usual with folk stories, several levels of understanding underpin this story: the surface story that uses nature and natural creatures as setting, the characters, and the fidelity of birds and their devotion to their chicks.

In the reincarnation, the birds change into a princess and a working man. The princess's refusal to talk, a result of events that happened when she was a bird, now challenges her former mate. He can win her back if he can persuade her to talk.

The former bird-husband, now a working-man suitor, seeks advice from the wise prophet. He succeeds in winning the princess and the couple marry. What had happened earlier provides a clue to solving the problem.

The lessons of fidelity, of the weak man's seeking help from the wise prophet, and of the couple's successful reconciliation teach the listener about hope and rewards.

Many birds mate for life. If you have ever watched birds build a nest, lay eggs, tend them, and feed the chicks until they fledge, you will know that the parent birds dedicate themselves to sharing the responsibilities and work of raising a family; such real-life dedication reinforces the story as an authentic fable.

Federal law protects swallows while these fleet birds raise their young by prohibiting the removal of nests (unless they are still under construction or have been vacated).

Of the eight swallow species in North America, barn swallows and cliff swallows regularly build nests under the eves of buildings, but sometimes this choice of nesting sites causes conflicts with people.

Personal Story

We once had a sad experience with nesting birds. Our dryer, which is in the basement, had a vent to the outside that emerges under the overhang of the house in an area surrounded by juniper bushes.

The efficiency of the dryer had fallen off gradually until the dryer no longer worked. We air-dried our clothes until our sons, handy with fixing our broken-down machines, could look at the dryer. We were all convinced that we had a defective heating element.

Rob and Eric checked the machine and decided that the problem was not with the element. They went outside to the exhaust tube and found it held a bird's nest containing three small white eggs.

When they had removed the nest, Rob and Eric went back to the dryer to try it out. It still didn't heat, so they removed the exhaust tube from the machine. After a lot of prodding and poking of long instruments through the tube, they finally found the problem: two swallows, a male and a female, huddled at the bottom of the tube. These parent birds had given their all to protect their nest and eggs.

This is a shocking example of the real extremes of nature. These faithful, dedicated birds gave their all for their family.

It was too late for this tragic bird family, but now a grill covers the exhaust opening.

The Sage Grouse
(Paiute)

Once upon a time, a long, long time ago, when mice ran after cats and rats chased lions, most of the world was under water except for the very tip of a mountain. Way up on top of the mountain, on its very tip, were the last remains of fire in the entire universe. This fire burned brightly on top of the mountain and flickered on the clouds in the sky.

The Paiutes, who had lived through the great storms and floods, knew that their only hope of survival was to get to the fire, which was high above them. But reaching the fire wouldn't be easy because storms raged and roared from the sky itself. Waves of water came close to putting out the fire.

Finally, when all the people had become depressed and had given up all hope, a little prairie chicken flew to the tip of the mountain and sat close to the fire. The bird fanned the fire to keep it alive. This brave little bird constantly protected the precious fire from the drenching waves of the flood as they swept and splashed near the fire.

The little bird fought the waves, fanned the fire, and was on the alert to danger. She managed to save the fire, but she paid dearly for her efforts. She had sat, danced, and fanned her wings so close to the fire that it scorched her breast—and to this day the little bird carries a black breast to remind everyone of her bravery and determination.

The words I have spoken, which you have now heard, you will hear tomorrow when a bird speaks them.

About the Story

Primitive cultures considered birds magical creatures. Unlike humans and other beasts, birds could sail to the heavens. Many cultures even worshipped birds and believed that they could bring rain, predict the future, and bring good or bad luck. Ojibway people tell a story explaining the reason grouse have spots on their tails. Their story has it that the eleven spots on the grouse's tail appeared when the bird would not do as it was told and as punishment it had to go without food for eleven days. The Cherokee people considered the meat of the birds taboo for pregnant women; they thought it bad luck because although this bird lays a large number of eggs, few of them hatch and fewer live to maturity.

The greater prairie chicken measures 16–18 inches long. It is a mottled brown and has a heavily barred breast and a white throat. The tip of the short, rounded tail has a wide black band.

The greater prairie chicken lives in native tall grass prairies and on some agricultural lands. Natural populations of the prairie chicken are shrinking as habitat disappears. Prairie chickens eat insects during summer and seeds and fruits during the winter.

Early March through the end of May is the best time to observe these birds in courtship display—a fascinating sight. When the male performs his mating dance, special inflatable air sacs on his chests emit a booming call, sometimes called drumming, that is audible for miles.

During courtship, each male claims a territory on the display ground, or *lek*. The male bows deeply, drops his wings, raises his neck feathers, and performs a dance of short steps and rapid foot stomping. Between surges of fancy footwork, the birds emit a gobbling sound followed by a laughing cackle. Dominant males with territories in the center of the lek do most of the breeding. Brief fights or face-offs occur when a male encroaches upon another males' territory.

Shortly after dawn, the males begin their strut, puffing out magnificent downy breasts and neck feathers and inflating two sacs that look like small balloons pushing out from their breasts. When they constrict them suddenly, they produce a distinct ker-plop, which attracts females. The male devotes his life to outlandish displays just to attract females for a few weeks the year.

When the birds take their leave from the courtship grounds a few hours after sunrise, their lively stage becomes once more an empty patch of prairie.

Colorado has six grouse species—sage, blue, sharp-tailed, ptarmigan, and greater and lesser prairie chicken. The sage grouse returns every year to the same bare patches of ground called leks (from the Scandinavian *leka*, meaning "to play"). British and American scientists have found that birds possess the kind of memory that enables people to recall where they left their car keys. Their research shows that birds can remember not only where, but also when they hid critical items such as worms and other food. The birds even dig up less perishable food if too much time has passed and their favorite worms have probably rotted. This memory is apparent with prairie chickens. Biologists tell of the birds returning to what was their former courting lek only to find it is now a road. They enact their courtship on the road—after all, isn't this their lek?

The birds depend on sagebrush for food, nesting, and shelter. For years, populations have declined because farmers and ranchers have used herbicides to clear brush. Cattle have overgrazed many areas, fires have destroyed grasslands, and roads have fragmented habitats.

These chicken-like birds have influenced the plains tribes of Native Americans, whose dancers take the design of their traditional feather decorations from the tail feathers of these birds.

Prairie chickens live life in a fine balance. Individual birds must look alike to predators but different from each other. Individuality in size and configuration may confer an advantage in attracting mates or intimidating competitors, but a bird that stands out from the rest of the group makes an easy target for predators and may not receive acceptance from the flock itself.

A female bird lays from 9 to 13 eggs per clutch; the baby birds leave the nest within hours of hatching. Within two days, the hatchlings hunt for insects by themselves. You might describe the flight of these birds as flap, fly, float, flap, fly, float.

Personal Story

One March day I read about a greater prairie chicken (or "Sandhill Dancers") viewing trip (see Figure 2.3, page 25), which took place during four weekends in March and April. The trips, sponsored by the Wray Museum, Colorado Division of Wildlife, and the Wray Chamber of Commerce, started in Wray, Colorado. I immediately contacted them and asked for information.

My husband, George, and I signed up for an expanded tour package, which included a tour of Wray Museum to acquaint the participants with the greater prairie chicken. The tour included a visit to the historic Crider Ranch, a steak fry with entertainment, a film and lecture program on the greater prairie chicken, motel lodging, early morning prairie chicken viewing, a chuck wagon breakfast at Kitzmiller Ranch, a tour of the Deterding Ranch and its exotic and native birds, a tour of the Wray fish hatchery, a tour of historic Beecher Island, a sack lunch, and transportation.

The tour director sent the following helpful list of things we would need: an alarm clock, warm clothes, binoculars, spotting scopes, cameras, camcorders, and anticipation.

Wray, on the main line of the Burlington-Northern Railroad at an elevation of 3,600 feet, lies 175 miles east from where we live and is on the headwaters of the Republican River, near the Kansas border.

North of Wray stretch sandhills; a picturesque line of buttes rises to the south. Many gulches and canyons lead up to and out onto the flats. The steep buttes rise about 175 feet above the Republican River.

After a quiet drive to Wray, we had enough time to make the first scheduled meeting at the Wray Museum. Even though it was April, it was cold! The weather reports predicted an unusual cold snap of minus 11 degrees for Saturday. With a bit of wind, it was good and cold, so we stopped off at a sporting goods store in Wray and stocked up on more wool socks and glove liners.

At the museum, the tour director turned us loose on the museum and its displays. Because Wray is so small, the museum surprised me with its size and the high quality of exhibits. Later that evening we toured Crider Ponds, formerly Long Ranch (homesteaded by George Long around the turn of the century). When the Criders purchased it, they developed it into a delightful park-like environment.

At the steak fry in Laird School, near the Crider Ponds, we saw a video called *Sandhill Dancers* and asked questions of two biologists from the Colorado Division of Wildlife. They were full of facts and legends about greater prairie chickens, and told us that it might not be a good idea to drink coffee and other liquids in the morning because once we got to the viewing trailer, we were there for the duration! There would be no potty breaks—there were no potty facilities! "We won't leave until the last hen does," one biologist warned us.

At 9:00 P.M. we returned to Wray and to our motel with strict instructions to meet at the motel parking lot at 4:00 A.M. for transportation to the lek. Twenty viewers (the maximum limit) made up our group.

The next morning at 4:00 A.M. the temperature had indeed plunged to minus 11 degrees. We piled into a small school bus and traveled out of town, onto dirt roads, and past other dirt roads, until the driver pulled in alongside a camouflaged metal trailer in a field. The trailer contained three levels of wooden benches and the entire front, which faced the field, opened. That trailer was cold. We all whispered as directed by the wildlife people. It was still dark, dark, dark. We sat there and waited.

Some of the avid birders in our group set up their cameras and nightscopes. We were told that we must not talk or move for fear of distracting the birds.

In the predawn darkness, we heard first the male prairie chickens flutter onto the lek. We heard them booming like bassoons. Then the meadowlarks began to sing, sounding like flutes. The effect was that of an orchestra tuning up.

As dawn lightened the sky, we could see bird figures strutting and booming and dancing. After 30 to 45 minutes the females came out of the grass and either chose mates and went off with them or said, "Forget it."

Our group included people from England and Sweden who had come especially for the tour. A mother and daughter had driven to Colorado from Pennsylvania just to see the prairie chickens.

And so we watched the males preening, bending forward, drooping their wings and fanning their tails. They stamped their feet while furiously bobbing over the prairie. At one point there must have been about 40 birds courting on the lek. The once-endangered prairie chicken numbered just 600 in Colorado 20 years ago; the population now exceeds 10,000.

Did I tell you it was cold? It was *sooooo* cold! The wooden benches warmed up from our body heat but the metal floor of the trailer never rose above minus 11 degrees. Our extra wool socks helped but . . . did I tell you it was cold?

When the last hen left, we stiffly climbed out of the trailer and into the bus. Did I tell you it was cold? We drove to the Kitzmiller Ranch for breakfast. The Kitzmiller Ranch consists of 15,000 acres and is owned by 34 members of a grazing association. Each member owns shares that represent a specific number of cattle. The grazing association group served us the most wonderful breakfast I have ever eaten, with special pig meat, which you can't buy in any store. The coffee was hot, hot, hot. Did I tell you it had been cold?

After breakfast we toured Deterding Ranch, located at the junction of the Republican River and Chief Creek. The owners raise exotic and native birds.

Next, we toured the Wray Fish Hatchery. The hatchery raises warm water fish and holds and distributes catchable trout. The trout hatching troughs have a capacity of 300,000 eggs; the hatchery supports 23 trout production ponds.

Then it was on to Beecher Island for a picnic lunch and a Native American storyteller. Beecher Island, on the Arickaree Fork of the Republican River, is the site where 75 Native Americans and five cavalrymen died in September of 1868 when about 500 Cheyenne, Arapahoe, and Sioux attacked in a dawn raid. When the Native Americans had completed several unsuccessful charges, they laid siege to the island and prepared to starve the soldiers out. The siege lasted nine days, when the soldiers were rescued by some of their own men, who had walked 100 miles to Fort Wallace for help. Chief Roman Nose and his medicine man were killed.

Shortly after we arrived home (George still complaining that he was cold), I saw an article about a weekend sage grouse tour at Walden in North Park. Walden lies 140 miles north and west from us, in the mountains. I begged George to go but he claimed that he had seen all the birds in the middle of the night that he planned to ever see. I signed up to go by myself the next weekend and see what explorers Lewis and Clark called the "Cock of the Plains."

This trip took place at the beginning of May. It followed the earlier prairie chicken tour with local home-cooked meals and hospitality. Again, we met in the motel parking lot for a 4:00 A.M. departure and traveled in vans to the lek. I guess I had fallen in love with the prairie chickens because these sage grouse seemed to lack some of the more delicate nuances of courtship. Maybe it was because the courtship season was coming to a close. Afterwards, we toured the wildlife resources and saw moose, waterfowl, shore birds, and birds of prey in bird and animal sanctuaries. The weather for this trip was not nearly as cold as the previous week—George would have loved it.

That spring I saw things I had never seen before and fell in love with prairie chickens and sage grouse—in spite of the cold (did I tell you it was cold?) and the memory of the Sandhill Dancers lingers fresh in my mind to this day.

Figure 2.2.   "The Sandhill Dancers" flyer.

Hummingbird's Trip
(Paiute)

In ancient times when the world was new, a rufous hummingbird decided that he wanted to see what was beyond the sun. Every day he watched the sun come up in one place of the sky and then go down in the opposite side of the sky. "There must be something special beyond the sun," he thought. "I need to know what it is."

So he thought of many ways to travel through the sky to find out what was beyond the sun. He thought, had ideas, changed them, and pondered how he could do such a thing. He finally settled on a plan.

He filled his pants full of seeds and started on his journey to see what the wonderful things might be that were beyond the sun. He ate only one seed a day as he made his trip. He flew and flew and flew. But one day he had to turn back because there were no more seeds in his pants.

And so, the rufous hummingbird came back home without ever finding out what was on the other side of the sun. He spent the rest of his life wondering, pondering, and dreaming about what might be beyond the wonderful sun that made its trip daily across the sky.

About the Story

Hummingbirds abound in Native American folktales and mythology. Many Central American peoples consider the hummingbird to have supernatural power. In a Brazilian story, a hummingbird hoarded water so that the people had no water at all and had to force the hummingbird to release the water.

All the stories about the hummingbird originate in the Americas because this is the only natural range for these small birds. Early explorers marveled at the tiny hummingbirds.

Huitzilopochitli, which means "hummingbird of the south," was an Aztec god of sun and war. Aztecs believed that dead soldiers were reincarnated as hummingbirds; they also believed hummingbirds were among the original creators of the world.

In Venezuela, the Arawak Indians tell how their ancestors obtained the first tobacco plants from Trinidad by sending a hummingbird perched on the back of a crane to snatch and bring back the jealously guarded seeds.

Taino Native American legend tells that hummingbirds were originally flies but the great father transformed them into birds. This Caribbean tribe considered the hummingbird the spreader of life on the planet because hummingbirds act as pollinators when they drink from one flower, inadvertently collect pollen, and then deliver it to the next flower as they move on to other blossoms.

A Mayan legend tells that birds who wanted the tribal wise man to show them how to build a nest were sent to the hummingbirds to learn. Hummingbirds, in another Mayan legend, were created after the great spirit had created all the other birds; when he had finished, he found that he had a pile of extra pieces left over, so he decided to make the tiniest bird of all. When he had created a pair of hummingbirds, he called all the other birds together to celebrate his work; the birds brought presents for the tiny hummingbirds. From the house finch, they received red feathers for a scarf for the male, who then gave several to his female partner. The hummingbird's feathers gleam and sparkle when the sun shines on them. The Portuguese named the hummingbird "flower kisser."

Many Central American peoples value the hummingbird as a love charm: they might wear a dead hummingbird around the neck in a little bag to gain the power to attract the opposite sex; they might also drop a little powder from a dried hummingbird into the drink of the person whose love they seek.

Some cultures see the hummingbird as the bringer of rain: Hopi and Zuni peoples include the hummingbird in their ceremonial rain dances and often use the birds to decorate water jars.

The ruby-throated hummingbird measures only three inches long; most hummingbirds are not even as long as a bald eagle's middle toe. The male ruby-throated bird has an iridescent scarlet throat patch, whitish gray belly and flanks, green back and crown, and a grayish black, forked tail.

The rufous hummingbird is only three and a half inches long. The rufous ranges farther north than any other hummingbird, and breeds as far north as southern Alaska. It prefers to winter in Mexico.

These birds inhabit meadows, clearings in forests, gardens, mountain parks, or wherever there are flowers; their migrations north coincide with the flowering of plants. Hummingbirds particularly love red flowers. The following plants can attract hummingbirds to your garden:

- Alcea rosea (hollyhock)

- Aquilegia (columbine)

- Asclepias tuberosa (butterfly weed)

- Clarkia (annual)

- Cleome hasslerana (spider flower/annual)

- Digitalis (foxglove)

- Indian paintbrush

- Lantana

- Lobelia cardinalis (cardinal flower)

- Monarda (bee balm)

- Penstemon

- Scarlet gilia

- Scarlet sage

- Veronica (speedwell)

- Zinnia (annual)

- Buddleia (butterfly bush)

Hummingbirds beat their wings from 70 to 80 times per second and up to 200 times a second during courtship flights. They can flap more than a million times without stopping. The wings rotate at the bird's shoulders, allowing the birds to make forward or backward strokes. Mixing these strokes—like treading water in midair—allows them to hover. They can whir at nearly 50 miles per hour. They are able to perch, but cannot walk.

Hummingbirds require high-energy food—sugar—from flowers or feeders but they also need protein and are active insect-catchers. They use their long tongues to draw the nectar from flowers.

The approximately 338 species of hummingbirds live an average of seven years and generally leave for their southern migration by the second week of September.

Personal Story

I first got a chance to observe hummingbirds up close and at leisure at our paradise in the mountains—our cabin. I hung a feeder on an aspen tree about five feet away from our cabin deck; the hummingbirds swarmed there. I watched these swift and agile stunt fliers hurtle downward in breathtaking nosedives, pull up suddenly into a hover, and change direction with stunning agility.

I also noticed aerial dogfights at the feeder: Some birds aggressively protected their food supply even when they had eaten their fill; indeed, great fusses and arguments erupted around that feeder.

A male rufous was in charge of the feeder. We called him Attila because of his aggressive behavior. The male rufous makes a distinct whirring noise as he dive-bombs the other hummingbirds and forces them toward the ground. Attila waged many dazzling and fierce battles; he was a skilled hit-and-run artist. How Attila zipped and flashed, and what a show he put on for us! He was superbird!

Each time we visited our cabin, I replenished the feeder before I did anything else; I was soon rewarded with a visit from Attila, who had perched nearby. I think he heard us coming and prepared himself for fresh food.

Then to my joy and shock, one day after I had put the feeder up, Attila swooped to me and gently kissed me on my cheek! That was the most amazing kiss I have ever had! After that first kiss, Attila always came to me in greeting.

I thought I even saw facial expressions on Attila when he was close to me; he certainly behaved like a dog as he followed me around. I could even hear him following me when I hiked in the mountains.

One sad summer, Attila did not appear. What had happened to him? Where did he go to winter? Had he made it? So many questions. No more Attilas visited our feeder. We still watch the flying jewels and their feats of navigation but never has another bird appeared like our dear Attila, the hummingbird.

Four-Footed Animals

"Something very ancient has nearly disappeared between humans and wild animals. We humans have lost the way for active engagement with wild species and the ability of a collective imagination to run wild beyond the confines of our settlements and constructs. I worry as wildlife slips out of sight, then out of mind, then out of dreams. A vacuum is created."

Bob Hernbrode, Colorado's statewide
coordinator for the Division of
Wildlife's Watchable Wildlife Program

COYOTES

Coyote and Fox
(San Luis Valley, Colorado)

Coyote was out in an open field chasing a field mouse from clumps of brush to tall grasses, but he could not catch him. Coyote was skittering around to make sharp turns when the mouse executed a neat quick change of direction. Fox was watching all this and shouted "Ooo-oo-ooo-hoo!"

Of course, Coyote found this taunting so upsetting that he became very angry and stopped chasing the mouse and instead took off after Fox.

Fox was prepared for this and led Coyote on a frustrating hunt. When Coyote caught up with Fox, he was startled to find Fox standing by a fire. Now, Fox had started the fire, but what was surprising was that Fox started to plead with Coyote not to eat him. "Please don't eat me. We are both in danger from the fire. The only way we can save ourselves is to climb into these two burlap bags."

"Why should I do such a thing?" asked Coyote.

Fox, however, convinced Coyote that they must hurry and save themselves. "Quick Coyote, get into this sack and I will tie you up and then I will get into the other one and tie the bag up myself. I know how to do this. Hurry! We must save ourselves."

Coyote was convinced by the urgency of Fox's actions and agreed. Fox threw one of the burlap bags over Coyote and tied it up. Being wily Fox, he threw the sack into the fire and ran away laughing.

Coyote managed to get out but not before he was painfully burned. Now he was really mad. "Just you wait Fox! I'm going to get you and you will be my supper!"

Coyote followed Fox's trail and found Fox holding up a huge boulder. "This rock is about to fall on us," panted Fox. "I am getting really tired of holding it up. I need to go get a drink from the lake. You hold it while I am gone so it doesn't fall on us."

Before he really thought about it, Coyote put his paws on the boulder and pushed and waited for Fox to return. The longer he held it, the angrier he got until Coyote decided he really didn't care if the rock fell or not. He let go of the rock and of course, it didn't fall. It never budged.

Coyote was furious and took off to find Fox; he vowed to make Fox suffer before he ate Fox for his succulent supper. Coyote loped off to the lake and just as he thought he would, he found Fox. He got ready to pounce on Fox.

"I'm sorry, Coyote," said Fox. "Wait. I have been trying to reach the cheese in the water to bring to you. I wanted to make it all up to you and bring you a gift." Fox pointed to the reflection of the moon in the still water of the lake.

Coyote was quite hungry by this time.

"Climb on the log," Fox told him. "I will push it near the cheese so you can get it."

Coyote did as Fox ordered and as soon as Coyote reached the end of the log, Fox tipped it over and "splash!" Coyote fell into the lake. If there is one thing that Coyote hates it is being in water, but even more than that, it is being tricked by Fox over and over again.

Coyote got to the shore and didn't even take time to shake himself. Beside himself with fury, Coyote took off after Fox. He dug his paw-nails into the ground as he once again vowed to do horrible things to Fox. Coyote found Fox quietly stirring a stick inside a beehive. Fox was very careful about the way he stirred.

"What are you doing now?" demanded Coyote.

"Sh! I am teaching school. Can't you hear my students reading?" answered Fox. "I am going to be paid a dozen fat hens for this. Do you want to teach for a while? Because I have sported with you, I'll make it up to you. You teach for a while and I will go get the fat hens and share them with you."

Greedy Coyote forgot his rage. All he could think of at this moment was how hungry he was. He could hear the students reading inside the beehive, so he felt safe. "All right. I'll teach them," and Coyote started stirring the beehive with the stick. He was very cautious with his stirring at first and then he got bored and gave the beehive a whack and the bees boiled out of the hive and stung him everywhere. They swarmed like a cloud around his head and stung him so badly that he could hardly see. Half-blind, hurting everywhere, and in a vengeful state of hostility, Coyote kicked up dust as he tore off after Fox.

Coyote found Fox calmly sitting and eating a watermelon. "I am eating half of this watermelon. That way it won't be so heavy to carry the other half to you," explained Fox. "Of course, I was going to bring your share to you but since you are here now, why don't you eat your half, Coyote?" Fox sounded so sincere. "In fact, Coyote, I'll get another watermelon tomorrow if you will get us another one the next night."

The watermelon patch belonged to an old couple. When they discovered some watermelons missing, they set up a scarecrow covered with tar. The next night when Fox came, Fox found the scarecrow and said to it, "Do you think I am afraid of you?"

Fox struck the scarecrow with his left paw and then when he couldn't get away, Fox kicked at the scarecrow with his hind feet. Fox was completely stuck.

The old couple found Fox stuck to the scarecrow and were about to kill him.

"Don't kill me," pleaded the Fox. "Coyote has been forcing me to steal. If you let me go and let me take a melon to Coyote, I'll get him to come to your watermelon patch himself tomorrow night." The Fox seemed so frightened of Coyote that the old couple agreed and set him free.

Fox returned to Coyote with the melon and bragged as he told Coyote all about the scarecrow. "It caught me but it was easy to get loose. You won't have any trouble with it tomorrow night."

Coyote went to the patch the next night and found himself the prisoner of the scarecrow covered with tar. He smacked the scarecrow to show how cool he was. When he got stuck, he smacked it with his other paw. He couldn't get any of his paws loose and his tail was even plastered tight into the tar. The old couple grabbed Coyote and strung him up on a tree and skinned him. They left only the hide on top of Coyote's head and on his paws.

"Never come back here again," they warned Coyote, and they let him go.

Coyote decided that he would never again have anything to do with Fox. Fox had gotten him into so much trouble, he was done with Fox forever. Fox was nearby and watched Coyote trotting away.

Fox started to laugh. "Goodbye, Coyote! You look so much better than when I first met you. Look at your handsome toupee and furry gloves." Coyote just kept on walking, wiser but certainly a different looking animal than when he first started to chase Fox.

About the Story

One of the most interesting characters among the Navajo is Coyote, the prince of chaos. He is called "Trickster" or "Trotting Coyote," a representation of socially unacceptable behavior. Coyote is a transformer, a troublemaker, a trickster, and a deity whose unruly behavior brings about changes. He comes from the Great Basin, the plains and plateau, and the southwestern Native American groups.

His changes make life better; for example, he stole the stars laid out by First Man and scattered them throughout the sky. He acts the court jester or wise fool, sacred and profane, and as such speaks and acts and creates new ways of doing things to clarify human and animal conduct.

Yes, he deceives; but he also brings newness and makes changes through his good and bad actions and reaffirms the eventual triumph of justice and morality.

Some coyote facts:

- Coyotes are omnivores and eat meat, vegetables, fruit and berries.
- The average coyote measures 37 inches long and 18 inches high, weighing from 20 to 50 pounds.
- Native Americans believe coyotes are the smartest animals on earth and refer to them as "God's dog".
- Coyotes are susceptible to rabies, but the disease is not prevalent.
- Coyotes begin breeding when they are two years old and can have up to 19 pups in a litter, although the average is from 3 to 5 pups per litter.
- Coyote pups stay with their parents no longer than two years before striking out on their own.
- Between 50 percent and 70 percent of coyote pups die before reaching adulthood because of trapping, car collisions and other accidents.
- Coyotes do not dig their own dens but instead use old fox or badger dens.

Again, Coyote stories serve to strengthen and reinforce moral values, social harmony, and cultural norms by endowing them with the prestige and power of antiquity as well as with the sanction and affirmation of the supernatural.

Coyote usually travels with a companion who could be Wolf, Wildcat, Fox, Rabbit, Porcupine, Badger, Lizard, or some other animal. In the folk stories, Coyote and his companion talk and behave like people. Coyote has been translated into the popular cartoon character, Wily E. Coyote.

Personal Story

As mentioned in the story, coyotes hate water. However, the following true story presents another side to Coyote:

We lived in Montana in the 1950s and became close friends (still are!) with Helen and Harry, a couple who lived nearby. Helen's father was the manager of a 14,000-acre cattle and sheep ranch.

When we visited this ranch one day, my friend's father showed us many wonderful things. At a remote spot on the ranch, we saw an Indian burial boulder and all sorts of beads and artifacts, which had fallen from bodies placed on the top of the rock. We saw hawks by the burial boulder; one even chased us off when we got too close to her nest, which she had built in a crack of the huge boulder. She protected her chicks with fury and determination.

Helen's father told us an amazing story: One day as he was out riding the fence line, he spotted a coyote gathering bits of sheep fleece that had been caught in the barbs of the fence. The coyote held these pieces of fleece in his muzzle and trotted off to the lake below. Then, to the watcher's amazement, the coyote slowly waded into the water up to his neck and then swam out farther. Eventually, Helen's father could see only the white blob of fleece above the water. After a while, the coyote left the fleece floating and swam away. He shook himself at the shore, rolled around on the ground, and then trotted off.

My friend's father couldn't stand the mystery of what he had just seen. He rode down to the lake and, using some branches from a nearby cottonwood tree, snagged the fleece and brought it to shore. To his surprise, fleas covered the fleece. That wily coyote had his own unique method of pest control.

One morning when I went for a walk in the local greenbelt, I crossed a wooden bridge that spanned Clear Creek and saw something off in the bushes. I followed the path that paralleled the movement in the bushes. To my pleasure, a coyote came out of the bushes and walked 15 yards ahead of me. He kept looking at me and walking to my side. We walked like this for a half mile to the lake. Then with a final look, he turned and trotted off to the rushes and reeds. I can now say that I have walked with a coyote.

I love the sounds of coyotes as they howl above our cabin in the mountains. I love thinking about one resourceful coyote with an amazing method of personal grooming and another coyote who walked with me.

WOLVES

The Wolf and the Seven Little Kids
(Jacob and Wilhelm Grimm)

Once upon a time, there was an old nanny goat who had seven little kids. She loved them with all the love of a mother for her children. One day she wanted to go into the forest and fetch some food, so she called all seven kids to her and said, "Dear children, I must leave you to go into the forest. Be on your guard against the wolf, for if he comes in, he will devour you—skin, hair, and all. The wretch often disguises himself, but you will know him at once by his rough voice and his black feet."

The kids said, "Dear mother, we will take good care of ourselves; you may go away without any anxiety." The old one bleated and went on her way with an easy mind.

It was not long before someone knocked at the door and cried, "Open the door, dear children, your mother is here and has brought something back with her for each of you."

But the little kids knew that it was the wolf, by his rough voice. "We will not open the door," cried they, "you are not our mother. She has a soft, pleasant voice, but your voice is rough; you are the wolf!" The wolf went away to a shopkeeper and bought himself a great lump of chalk. He ate the chalk and made his voice soft with it.

Then he came back, knocked at the door of the house, and cried, "Open the door, dear children, your mother is here and has brought something back with her for each of you."

But the wolf had laid his black paws against the window, and the children saw them and cried, "We will not open the door. Our mother does not have black feet like you: you are the wolf!"

Then the wolf ran to a baker and said, "I have hurt my feet; rub some dough over them for me." And when the baker had rubbed the wolf's feet, the wolf ran to the miller and said, "Rub some white flour over my feet for me." The miller thought to himself, "The wolf wants to deceive someone," and refused, but the wolf said, "If you will not do it, I will devour you." Then the miller was afraid, so he made the wolf's paws white for him.

Now the wretch went for the third time to the house door, knocked at it, and said, "Open the door for me, children! Your dear little mother has come home, and has brought each one of you something back from the forest with her."

The little kids cried, "First show us your paws that we may know if you are our dear little mother." Then the wolf put his paws up to the window, and when the kids saw that they were white, they believed that all he said was true and opened the door. But who should come in but the wolf!

The kids were terrified and tried to hide themselves. One sprang under the table, the second into the bed, the third into the stove, the fourth into the kitchen, the fifth into the cupboard, the sixth under the washing bowl, and the seventh into the clock case. But the wolf found them, and used no great ceremony; one after the other, he swallowed them down his throat. The youngest, who had hidden in the clock case, was the only one he did not find. When the wolf had satisfied his appetite he took himself off, lay down under a tree in the green meadow outside, and went to sleep.

Soon afterwards the old mother goat came home again from the forest. What a sight she saw there! The door of the house stood wide open. The table, chairs, and benches were thrown down, the washing bowl lay broken to pieces, and the quilts and pillows were pulled off the bed. She sought her children, but they were nowhere to be found. She called them one after another by name, but no one answered. At last, when she came to the youngest, a soft voice cried, "Dear mother, I am in the clock case." She took the kid out and it told her that the wolf had come and eaten all the others. Then you may imagine how she wept over her poor children.

At length in her grief she went out and the youngest kid ran with her. When they came to the meadow, there lay the wolf by the tree, snoring so loudly that the branches shook. The mother goat looked at the wolf on every side and saw that something was moving and struggling in his gorged body. "Ah heavens," said she, "is it possible that my poor children, whom he has swallowed down for his supper, can be still alive?"

Then the kid ran home and fetched scissors and a needle and thread. The mother goat began to cut open the monster's stomach. Hardly had she made one cut that one little kid thrust its head out. When she cut farther, all six sprang out one after another. They were all still alive and had suffered no injury whatever, for in his greediness the wolf had swallowed them down whole. What rejoicing there was! They all embraced their dear mother and jumped for joy all around the meadow.

The mother, however, said, "Now go and look for some big stones, and we will fill the wicked beast's stomach with them while he is still asleep." Then the seven kids dragged large stones to their mother with all speed, and put as many of them into the wolf's stomach as they could get in. The mother sewed him up again in the greatest haste, so that he was not aware of anything and never once stirred.

When the wolf at length had had enough sleep, he got to his feet and decided to go to a well to drink, as the stones in his stomach made him very thirsty. But when he tried to walk and to move about, the stones in his stomach knocked against each other and rattled. Then he cried,

What rumbles and tumbles
against my poor bones?
I thought 'twas six kids,
But it's naught but big stones.

When the wolf got to the well, he stooped over the water and was just about to drink when the heavy stones shifted and made him fall in. There was no help and the old wolf drowned miserably. When the seven kids saw that, they came running to the spot and cried aloud, "The wolf is dead! The wolf is dead!" and danced for joy round about the well with their mother.

Figure 3.1   Wolves statue at Denver Museum of Natural History.

About the Story

Western European folklore and language has stereotyped wolves for thousands of years. Figures of speech, such as "wolf in sheep's clothing," "wolf whistle," "cry wolf," "wolf pack," "wolf your food down," "lone wolf," and "she-wolf," demonstrate the negative value judgments humans have placed on wolves. Many of these wolf references can be found in collections of Aesop's fables.

The Bible uses the wolf as a symbol of evil: "Beware of false prophets, who come to you in the clothing of sheep, but inwardly they are ravening wolves" (Matthew 7:15); "Behold, I send you as sheep in the midst of wolves" (Matthew 10:16);

"I know that after my departure, ravening wolves will enter among you, not sparing the flock" (Acts 20:29). According to the Bible, wolves are vicious, false, and evil. The kindest thing the Bible has to say for the wolf appears in Isaiah 11:6: "The wolf and the lamb will lie down together and the leopards and goats will be at peace. Calves and fat cattle will be safe among lions, and a little child shall lead them all." As far as kindness goes, the wolves are categorized with leopards and lions—all of them obviously dangerous.

In pre–Christian Europe, however, the wolf became a popular clan totem. People who claimed the wolf as an ancestor believed that, with the invocation of specific sacred rites and rituals, they could become wolves or be turned into wolves. The ancient Egyptians referred to their the wolf god, Up-Uat (who predated Horus and Anubis), as "Opener of the Way" or "Opener of the Body." The early Roman cult of Lupa worshipped The Great Goddess as the "great she-wolf." She was the "Mother of the Wolves," the divine midwife, the mother of the ancestral spirits; she was also foster mother to Romulus and Remus, the twins who founded Rome. Numerous folk stories include similar tales of a nurse wolf who nurtures human children.

The wolf, an omen of death, symbolizes winter and darkness. The Germanic gods donned wolf skins to signify the solar hero hidden by the night or the dark of winter; they removed the wolf skins to signify the light of day and spring. The wolf of evening succeeds in his wickedness, swallowing the hero and taking him into the underworld; this wolf is foiled by the brilliance of the rising hero of the dawn. The morning wolf and the springtime wolf triumph until vanquished by the evening and winter wolves; thus they describe the ancient cycles.

This duality may explain the diverse characteristics ascribed to the wolf in common lore. On the one hand, the good wolf defends the faith and the faithful and enjoys curative powers. For example, beliefs held that wolf teeth rubbed over the gums of teething children relieved pain; that wearing a wolf's head brought courage; that wearing a wolf skin made children strong and brave; and that a wolf's bite rendered one invulnerable and impervious to pain. On the other hand, the diabolical and perfidious wolf reigned as king of wickedness and perversity: we see him portrayed as a thief on the road; an evil, malignant spirit; and a fraudulent, double-dealing, deceiving beast capable of witchcraft and murderous intent.

Other folk beliefs concerning wolves include the following:

- To sleep well, put a wolf's head under the pillow.

- A wolf skin coat guards its wearer against hydrophobia (rabies).

- Sprinkle salt in a wolf's tracks to keep the wolf away.

- Wolf's milk purifies the skin.

- To be seen by a wolf before you see the wolf means that you will lose your powers of speech.

- To make a wolf drop a stolen livestock animal, drop an object from your pocket.

• Saying the name of the wolf even once during the twelve days of Christmas invites the wolf to your door.

In European folk tales, the werewolf lives as a person by day and a wolf by night, possibly the victim of a wicked enchantment. At daybreak, the wolf hides his wolf's coat. Some stories tell that it is possible to break such a spell by pointing at the werewolf while he is in his human form and shouting, "You are the wolf!" However, the enchantment may rebound to the accusing person.

Native American folk beliefs show a more positive image of the wolf. The Wolf Clan is one of the eight clans of the Seneca. For some tribes, the Wolf Spirit is a teacher who offers many lessons for those willing to look beyond physical boundaries; the Wolf Spirit sings the moon into the sky. Native Americans respect the wolf because of its family ties and social nature. Wolves also cooperate as hunters, know how to survive, and provide well for their families.

After fierce fighting at Sand Creek, Colorado, on November 29, 1864, the phantom of a gray wolf is said to have appeared to the surviving Cheyenne women and children to lead them to safety. The mysterious animal escorted the few survivors all the way to another Cheyenne camp, near the forks of the Smoky Hill and Republican Rivers.

Description

The wolf resembles a large German shepherd dog, with longer legs and larger feet than its domesticated cousin (see Figure 3.2, page 40). Other differences include stronger jaws, a wider head, ears that always stand up straight, and a long, bushy tail. Male wolves weigh more than 100 pounds (45.4 kilograms) and they can travel for hours at about 20 miles (32 kilometers) per hour.

Wolves may be white, gray, brown, or black. Generally, wolves of the northern and arctic regions are lighter in color than those of the southern forests. The arctic wolf, which may be pure white, has often bred with domestic dogs to produce a strong, hardy sled dog. Two species of wolf are native to North America: the gray wolf (or timber wolf) and the red wolf. Scientists have identified 32 subspecies of the gray wolf in North America.

Wolves maintain strong family ties and they often mate for life. Two months after mating, usually in April or May, the female gives birth to four to six pups in a den she has dug in the earth; the pups are blind for about a week after birth. Both wolf parents feed and train the pups, who remain with the family group for quite a while; in fact, wolf packs are simply family groups. Wolves communicate with each other through their howls. Jim Bridger, American pioneer and scout in the late 1880s, noted that wolves signal to each other and understand each other in a manner similar to that of human beings.

Wolf pups spend their days chasing grasshoppers, field mice, and gophers. Although they also eat smaller mammals and rodents, wolves in the wild usually prey on caribou, moose, and deer, selecting weaker animals for their meals. Wolves form a vital part of the natural community. Because they kill sick or injured animals, they keep caribou, moose, and deer herds in a healthy condition. As humans move into their territory, bringing with them domestic animals, the wolf has added cattle and sheep to its diet. Wolves prefer to live in forested areas with thick brush. The name *timber wolf* indicates the wolf's presence in heavily wooded regions.

Figure 3.2 Wolf tracks.

Personal Story

Dogs are descended from wolves. In a recent study, University of California (Los Angeles) biologist Robert Wayne compared the DNA of wolves, dogs, and other canines around the world; the study showed that dogs have evolved from wolves and that the domestication of wolves began as early as 135,000 years ago. Throughout the ages, man has bred dogs for desired physical and behavioral features. Domestic dogs faithfully serve their masters; indeed, many descendants of the wolf have enriched and blessed our family.

When we lived in Montana, our next door neighbor worked on a local ranch. One day, the neighbor came over with a tiny puppy. The ranch dog had given birth to a litter of puppies, and right after their birth had been killed when she went out to chase a car on the dirt road. Our neighbor was looking for homes for the pups. Our daughter, Lauren, had just fallen in love with some Kipling stories we read her about the God Nong. She decided to name the dog Nong, but when she said it, it came out "Pong"—so Pong it was.

What a dog! We raised Pong on eyedroppers of milk, and obviously he was imprinted on our family. What a loyal dog he was—and how like his mother. We found out later that she was an Australian sheep dog and like her, Pong wanted to herd every car he ever saw. One day, poor Pong was hit by a truck on a nearby dirt road, which left him with a dead tail. What a sight to watch him run with his dead tail flapping!

Pong helped me with baby-sitting. When, in Pong's judgment, baby Rob wandered too close to the road, Pong knocked him down and dragged him back to where he felt Rob would be safe.

One of our nearby neighbors came to the front door one day with the plea to take Pong into the house. Our neighbor was intent on cutting a switch from the willow tree in his yard to administer some punishment to his kids, but Pong grabbed the neighbor's wrist with every swing and refused to let him strike the kids. I laughed and told our neighbor that his kids had probably had enough fear in their hearts from the entire process and that it was good to know that Pong protected all our children. There was no punishment that day.

One day I was putting the twins and baby Rob to bed for an afternoon nap; when I had settled the children, I could not find four-year-old Lauren. Oh swell! There was a road out front, a field full of bucking broncs down below, a welding company on the other side, and railroad tracks, which were rarely used, on the other.

Pong greeted me at the door, took me by the wrist, and led me half a mile away to a smiling Lauren, who was sitting on a barrel watching the "horsies" in the fenced field. What a dog! Lassie couldn't have done better.

What a dog indeed. He slept under our bed. The springs were bare—no plush elaborate cover on mattress springs in those days. Once, in the middle of the night, Pong caught his healthy collie coat in the springs and let out some terrified yelps. Being awakened in the middle of the night by banshees, I automatically jumped straight into action because I was bouncing on the bed, screaming. Each time I bounced, the banshees screeched while a not fully awake husband was sitting upright in bed watching his screaming wife using the bed as a trampoline and hearing unholy noises from below, all the while yelling, "What, what, what, what the _____ is going on?" Ah yes, what a dog.

Another Pong story from this time: When we took vacation trips to Canada to visit husband George's folks, we usually boarded Pong at the kennel because he tried to herd other cars on the road from inside our car. Trips with him were not fun. On this trip we were planning to be away for three weeks for the first time. When we returned to Montana and went to the veterinarian's to collect Pong, we found a nearly dead dog. He had refused to eat or drink and, in the third week, he became dehydrated, dazed, and starved. We took him home, but it was hours before he revived and realized that we were all back together. What a wild celebration he had when he came out of his shock!

Four years later, we were living in Pennsylvania. Pong had a monumental hatred of mail carriers in general and one mail carrier in particular. Once, with Pong chained in the yard, the mail carrier went out of his way to kick our dog. We had to have Pong's ears surgically fixed as a result of the damage from the kicking. Pong got his revenge one day, though, when he had managed to run loose outside just when the mail carrier approached our house. Pong performed the proverbial bite-in-the-seat-of-the-pants; the mail carrier dropped his mailbag and took off. I stood by the mailbag wondering whether I should finish the route for the afflicted mail carrier. I might add that we didn't receive mail delivery for some time after that.

It was also during this time that our youngest child, Rob, felt the world was cruel to him; he would go out to Pong's doghouse, crawl in with him, and tell Pong all his troubles. I discovered this one day when I saw Rob going out to the doghouse. I circled the doghouse and eavesdropped; never have I felt such sympathy for Rob, and how sorry I was that I had given him such problems. Pong was certainly a cheap psychiatrist.

Some time after we had adopted Pong, we inherited my Dad's basset hound, Nutsy. We decided to breed Nutsy and get rich selling puppies, so we paid an expensive stud fee to breed her. The stud owner said he had never seen such a vicious dog—she refused the advances of his stud in a very savage manner. When we tried again later with the same results, we christened her "the virgin." What we didn't know was that she was really saving her affections for Pong. Their litter of three pups was something to behold!

On another trip to Canada from Pennsylvania, Pong and Nutsy became legends. We had learned to give Pong tranquilizer pills the vet had prescribed to make him sleepy while we traveled. That solved the problem of his tireless yelping barks and bounding off the windows, seats, ceiling, and people in his efforts to protect us from the dangers of approaching or following cars. Nutsy was no problem. She just dropped to the car floor and slept—unless the car went up and down hills; then she just dropped to the car floor and vomited.

The first 600 miles of the trip had been peaceful while Pong slept and Nutsy took turns sleeping and vomiting. Just before we crossed into Canada, a skunk committed suicide by running into our moving car in the middle of a pouring rain. The smell of wet, fresh skunk juice is powerful. At the Canadian border, the border guards didn't even questioned our car's occupants; they just held their noses and motioned the Livo car to keep moving (we had accidentally discovered how to make customs checks at the border crossing quick and easy).

That night we settled down in a cozy mom-and-pop motel on the outskirts of town. The motel owners had a female collie, Suzy, who romped with our kids and dogs that evening. In the morning when we loaded up the car, I put Pong in the front seat and gave him his restful pills and stroked his throat to help the pills go down smoothly. Nutsy, in preparation for the trip, had already collapsed on the floor like a long sack of rocks. I assigned window seats to the youngsters who were "next" in line for a window. About five miles from the motel, the pills started to take effect. Pong's eyes crossed, his legs wouldn't support him, and he started to buckle. His bark lost its sharpness. He was going down.

Then it happened! The Royal Mounted Canadian Police were lurking around a bend in the road. We drove by them, followed by three other cars. We saw the police car pull onto the road. No problem—no one was speeding. And so it went for another ten miles. Then the police car passed the three cars in front of it and lit its lights and sirens. They motioned us over. When both cars had stopped, the officers approached both sides of our car with drawn weapons—guns. "Let me see your driver's license and owner's papers for the car," said the officer by the driver's side. Meanwhile the other officer by my side told me to remain calm. (Calm? Remain calm?) "What does calm mean?" asked the children. I replied, "Hush children. Be calm." Bright, eh?

The first officer took the papers back to the police car to radio in the information. The other officer started frowning and looking at our car questioningly. "Where's the skunk?" he asked as he tried to get to a comfortable distance from our fragrant car. "It was an American skunk," my husband told him. No smiles.

More questions from the kids: "Will they put us in jail?" "What did we do, Daddy?" "Is killing a skunk bad?" "Can I go to the bathroom, Mommie?" After a long time the officer returned with the papers. He handed them back to George and asked, "Do you have a dog with you?"

"Of course we do," answered George. Nutsy was asleep on the floor and Pong was trying to focus his eyes but was unable either to focus or to bark. He looked pathetic with his drooping crossed eyes and a confused look of panic on his face. "Yes, we have two dogs, officer, and I have their papers here." We knew enough to have the dogs vaccinated and to bring along the papers as proof. George gave the papers to the policeman.

By now the police guns were back in their holsters but the officers were both trying to keep upwind of our perfumed car. The officer returned to the police car to radio the dog information. When he returned after what seemed like a really, really long time, the other officer had walked quite a distance ahead of our car. The kids said nothing all this time, save for the occasional question and request to go to the bathroom. The situation created nervous bladders even in the young.

This time when the officer returned, he told us we could go. "We are looking for a ring of dognappers operating in this area. Someone kidnapped Suzy back at the motel where you stayed and a woman reported seeing you with dogs and putting something into one of them."

"Well, officer, I could have saved you a lot of time. If you had only told us that at the beginning, I could have turned Pong over and you could see for yourself that his name couldn't be Suzy," George told him.

Then Robbie piped up from the back seat, "I saw the people that took Suzy. They were driving a blue Chevrolet they went the other way on the road."

With this information, the officers pulled out with flying clots of mud, leaving us, the sleeping dogs, the aromatic car, and the jiggling children. Three weeks later on the return trip of our vacation, we stopped by the mom-and-pop motel and inquired about Suzy. "Yes," the owners told us, "Suzy was found and the dognappers were caught. A little boy gave the police the information that led them to the capture."

Moral of the story #1: Don't let skunks commit suicide on your car in the rain at night—it stinks.

Moral of the story #2: Look out for little ladies peeping out of their motel windows when you give sleeping pills to hyperactive and protective dogs.

Moral of the story #3: Always ask little boys questions about dogs. It will save time.

We finally lost Pong when he was 17 years old. He chased one last car while the kids and I were on a camping trip outside of Steamboat Springs. He had suffered a stroke earlier, so he may have been confused when he left our tent. We buried him up on the pass with a pine tree over his grave. Every time we travel over that pass we give greetings to one wonderful dog—or was he really a protective wolf?

ELK

"The Gift of the Elk"
(This is a Lakota tale Charles Eagle Plume told me,
retold here with his permission.)

A young warrior with long braided hair loved a special young girl. He was a poor orphan youth without family or a lodge of his own.

He loved one of the village maidens but was shy about telling her of his love. After all, who was he, an orphan boy with nothing to offer? One morning, he met the maiden at the watering place and told her of his love for her. She just laughed at him and said, "Who do you think you are? Why should I marry someone who lives among the tents, someone without a home?" She went on to insult and revile him. "I am the daughter of the chief, and who are you?" Her manner toward him was haughty and arrogant.

The rejected fellow was full of shame. "It would be just as well if I died now. There is nothing for me here in this village," he thought.

At dawn, the warrior shot an arrow northward and walked after it. He walked until evening and was just about to stop and rest when he discovered a fat deer impaled by his arrow. He cut up the deer and roasted a piece of the meat. When he had eaten, the hurt in his heart eased, and because he was tired, he soon fell asleep beside the fire.

It went like that for four days. The young warrior would shoot an arrow at dawn, find a deer killed by the arrow in the evening, butcher the animal, cook the meat, and eat it. At last, he felt a little more cheerful.

On the fourth evening, as he sat alone by the fire, the boy thought, "I might as well go back home to the village." Then a strange sound came to him from a grove of trees. He thought he heard human voices. Expecting the worst, he thought, "What if they do kill me? There is nothing left for me. In fact, didn't I come this way seeking death?"

The voices drew nearer and he recognized the language they were speaking. "They are speaking Lakota," he thought.

There were two voices. One of them said, "Friend, you give it to him," but then the other voice replied, "No, friend, you give it to him." The first voice spoke again, "Friend, you tell him properly." Again the other speaker refused. "But no, friend, you tell him." At last the two speakers stopped just within the circle of firelight, and the boy saw an amazing thing.

There before him were two men. They were the handsomest young men he had ever seen. As they stood there in front of him, their bodies seemed to emit a glimmering and glowing light.

After a long silence, one spoke: "Boy, we know that you have much pain in your heart, but this will never be so a second time. Listen closely." They had with them a long wooden flute and one of them began to play.

The youth heard a sweet piercing sound come from the flute. The man playing the flute held it out to the boy. "Take this with you and go home. At midnight when the people are sleeping, walk through the camp playing this flute, and you will find that all the women will get up and follow you." The two handsome men turned around, and before the astonished youth's eyes, he saw two elk disappear among the trees.

The boy returned home to his village. It was late when he got there and everyone was asleep. He walked among the tents playing the flute. As the music filled the air, the women all got up from their beds and began to follow him, dragging their blankets behind them. They crowded around him, but he ignored them all. He was enchanted by the wonderful music he was playing.

From among the women one slender young maiden stepped out in front of him and repeatedly asked him, "Don't you remember me? I am the chief's daughter." But strangely the young man only heard the sound of the wonderful music that came from the mouth of the flute.

One girl of all the women in the camp didn't join the throng of women. She was sitting alone quietly in her lodge. It was she that the youth sought out and married.

It is said that this is the story of the gift of the courting flute.

About the Story

Elk live in forests, mountain meadows, and foothills in the Rocky Mountain region. They are from four to five feet broad at the shoulders and weigh from 400 to 900 pounds. Elk are reddish brown in summer, tannish brown in winter, with a dark mane and creamish rump patch. Males have large racks of antlers, which extend over their backs rather than pitching forward like a deer's antlers. They feed on grasses, shrubs, and sedges (see Figure 3.3).

Many Native American stories show respect and reverence for the elk; in their stories, as in "The Gift of the Elk," the elk gives the courting flute to people. Native Americans call elk "wapiti," which means "white rump."

Personal Story

On many of our travels we have seen elk browsing as we watched from our car (see Figure 3.3). We have seen elk resting in ravines beside the road, chewing their cud and quietly looking around. On hikes, we have developed a habit of sitting quietly with our backs against the perfect tree; a variety of critters passing by, even elk, have rewarded us during these pleasant moments of silence. We have even seen a dozen elk browsing on a miniature golf course (see Figure 3.4). Their scat was the vision of a new game of miniature golf!

We spot elk regularly in the foothills near our home. When I was recuperating from a major physical crisis, my husband, George, used to drive me to this

Figure 3.3   Grazing elk. Photo by Norma J. Livo.

Figure 3.4   Elk on a miniature golf course. Photo by Norma J. Livo.

area; there we would sit and watch a herd of elk. I am sure that this was more healing for me than much of the medicine I had to take.

The rutting season for elk, with the eerie whistling grunts of bull elk calling any challengers while charming a harem of cows, starts in the middle of September. Witness this ritual and feel the magic!

One special event for our family occurred late one September. We had rented several cottages in a resort near the Rocky Mountain National Park for four days. The 16 members of our family hiked, swam, rode horses, fished, attended cowboy dinners, and swapped stories. One night, I gathered a group who wanted to spend the evening in the Rocky Mountain National Park at Elk Meadow; there we would view and listen to the herd of elk that had come down from the hills for the rutting season.

We collected kids, blankets, and some munchy refreshments and drove into the park. A bright half-moon shone on the meadow. But there was more. Parked cars lined the road overlooking the meadow, and vehicles cruised by. Radios blared. Noisy talk and laughter pierced the still evening. Car lights flashed down the road and car doors slammed shut as people found places to stop.

We had arrived early enough to find a grassy place overlooking the scene—the meadow was filled with elk. We had spread out blankets hoping to observe the ritual in peace. As the evening wore on, more traffic filled the road. People stood all along the road and the elk gathered only 50 yards away.

Then, to our horror, one young woman took her two toddlers by the hands and started to lead them straight into the meadow, aiming for the biggest bull elk there. Until then, the elk were oblivious to the people observing. When bystanders saw this woman and children advancing on the elk, they started shouting orders to her to get herself and the children out of there quickly. The elk stopped their natural events to watch this woman and her young ones. A bull elk's anger can be fierce when his amorous mood is challenged, but fortunately the woman recognized the urgency of the commands from the viewers and retreated.

We quickly explained to our grandchildren why this woman's actions were foolish. "She's been to too many zoos," one of our grandchildren pronounced. And so the evening went on with all the noise and lights of humans. As people became bored and left the meadow, we stayed snug in our blankets and whispered to each other.

The elk whistled, danced, and performed their "king of the hill" behavior by the light of the moon. Off to the sides, just inside the wooded area around the field, the coyotes started their singing, too. I will always remember that night for its incredible beauty and for its demonstration of people out of touch with the natural world around them.

An elk footnote: In June 1998, our family had just spent a lovely evening dining at Wild Basin Lodge. We left the lodge to return to the Elkhorn Ranch, where we were staying in Estes Park, Colorado. It was just before dusk and I was driving the lead car; suddenly, the most magnificent elk bull I had ever seen crossed the road right in front of me. I stopped to admire him (and of course to let him cross the road safely) until he disappeared into the woods on the other side. We all agreed that this vision was a gift to our family and one of the highlights of our trip. Our daughter later presented me with a fist-sized rock with an image of the elk we had seen carved in it. I treasure that memento of our trip.

WEASELS

The Weasel and the Mouse
(Aesop)

A very lean and hungry little mouse crawled through a small crack into a corncrib. Once in there, he ate and nibbled and munched until he had eaten his fill. His stomach was swollen with corn and the little mouse was content for the first time in quite a while.

Meanwhile, as the little mouse ate his fill, Weasel heard the munching and contented eating sounds the little mouse made. Weasel discovered the crack in the corncrib and stationed himself beside it.

The full little mouse came to the crack in the corncrib he had entered earlier. He was able to get his head through the hole, but the rest of his body was now too large to make it through the small crack. He quickly pulled his head back into the corncrib, though, when he saw Weasel waiting there.

Weasel laughed and started to give advice to the mouse. "Don't worry little one. You will get out all right when you become lean again." And so the amused Weasel played the role of adviser to the mouse.

About the Story

Successive generations constantly add to the stories of human thought contained in the world's literature. Great thoughts never die; they are inspiration born of genius and they live from age to age, enriching the generations of all time. Great thoughts appeal to some universally shared instinct or truth. One of the most ancient, interesting, and useful methods of instilling moral instruction was through allegory, parable, or fable. A fable is an ingenious method of conveying advice and instruction without seeming to do so; it is a diverting little narrative that leads to a moral.

Aesop is the most famous creator of fables. A saying goes that one touch of nature makes the whole world kin; Aesop used touches of nature in his universally appealing stories.

According to scholars, Aesop was a native of Phrygia, born a slave. His sage advice directed his countrymen to measures that gave them their liberty. With a single fable, it is said, he baffled Croesus, King of Lydia. Aesop had several masters but his last master, Idmon, was so well pleased with Aesop that he gave him his freedom.

Some compare Aesop to the Seven Sages of Greece. Legend has it that Chilo, one of the wise men of Greece, asked Aesop, "What was God doing?" Aesop replied, "He was humbling the proud and exalting the humble."

The Delphians accused Aesop of sacrilege and convicted him through an act of the greatest villainy. The Delphians had concealed among Aesop's baggage, at his departure from Delphi, some golden vessels consecrated to Apollo, and then dispatched messengers to search his baggage; they accused him of theft and sacrilege, condemned him, and flung him over a rock to his death.

Personal Story

In 1986 I woke up one morning to horror—I was blind in my right eye!! Absolutely and totally blind. Of course, I went to the doctor, who told me that I had a central retinal vein occlusion—the vein had burst and covered my retina with blood.

The glorious fall weather was inviting. I decided to take the Jeep and spend a day in the mountains. I had two purposes: I wanted to see how one-eyed driving went, and I wanted to take some photographs. Photography had been a pleasurable hobby of mine, and I was concerned because I had always used my right eye to focus my 35-millemeter camera. I realized that I had several new habits to develop that my new vision limitations dictated.

I successfully (and with some growing confidence) drove up to the mountains. I took the steep, narrow shelf road to our cabin, a challenge with both eyes working. After opening the cabin, I hiked up the road with my camera. The following story is an article I wrote about my amazing experience with nature. Aesop could have added to it with another fable, I am sure.

Getting Ready for Winter

Harvest time is coming and the animals of the wild prepare carefully. The squirrels collect pine cones and other available goodies. The stellar jays raucously demand the crumbs and peanuts we place on the rock outside our mountain cabin. We sit on the deck and watch them gather the treats and stash them away. The jays glide in, pick up their good gifts, and wing away to the trees by a nearby stream. They deposit their loot in the crotch of branches or under the tree bark and swoop back for more.

Late fall trips to Mt. Evans find the mountain goats shedding their old coats for new winter coats. Their shaggy covering resembles that of some bag lady from downtown Denver.

The aspen trees get their leaves ready for their glorious seasonal binge of color and light. The leaves start turning nearest the trunk and then the change spreads out to the tips of the branches. The golden offerings dance in the crisp breeze and are enriched by the deep blue of the sky. In these resplendent forests the elk bugle announces the coming of winter. They are advertising their territory and their calls are another signal for us humans of the passing of the seasons.

Up above the 9,000 foot level, the marmots, or whistle pigs, are taking their last sunbaths of the season. When approached, they whistle a shrill warning to each other.

If you observe and are patient, many of these mountain creatures can be caught in the act of preparing for winter. During a recent October, I was treated to the food-gathering actions of a new, to me, small critter. I was hiking in the woods above Eldora, crunching leaves underfoot and absorbing the peace. I spied movement near a large boulder and went over to check it out. Hiding on the other side of the rock was a reddish brown weasel. He peeked out at me and then quickly ducked back. We skirmished around the rock and then he dashed up the hill. I hung around the rock and was pleased to see him returning down the hillside with a large vole (a small tail-less rodent that averages from four to six inches in length) in his mouth. When he again noticed me, he dropped his banquet and disappeared farther downhill. Now I had him. I had his vole, so I waited. Sure enough, he scampered back up to me but surprised me by continuing past me and the dropped vole. When I saw him again, he was heading downhill with a second vole in his mouth.

He returned shortly and headed up the hill again. And then raced down with yet a third vole. I was beginning to wonder how many voles he had stashed away. I felt certain that he would eventually be back for the vole I was guarding. Sure enough, this time he edged near to the rock and the abandoned vole. He stopped, stared at me with his pussycat face and prepared to battle this monster for the vole. He jumped behind the vole, and assumed an attack stance. When no attack came from me, he grabbed our vole and tore off with it.

Maybe somewhere this winter, up above 9,000 feet and under the snow, the weasel has again filled his larder and is surviving the winter by crunching on delicious vole bones and flesh. I'll also rationalize the fact that there are at least three voles that won't have to worry about where their food is coming from.

"Getting Ready for Winter" by Norma J. Livo, *Colorado Outdoors,* September/October, 1987, 23.

Footnote

This article makes no mention of my blindness and the need for this trip. However, this incident was an absolute gift to me. I shot pictures of the various events with the weasel and our vole. I used my left eye to focus and I fumbled, but I shot pictures.

Yes, the pictures turned out less than sharp (see Figure 3.5), but the weasel was distinguishable. I had these images blown up to 14-by-16 inches and framed. This day, this trip, and this event gave me more therapy and courage than I could ever have dreamed of. I knew life would go on—it would not be perfect but still exciting surprises waited around every corner. Aesop would have liked that!

Since this story was symbolic for me in my new blindness, isn't it a coincidence that my weasel was stashing away voles? Voles are blind!

Figure 3.5   Weasel with vole. Yes, this photo of the weasel and vole is not in the best of focus, but when you read my personal story, you will see why I treasure it. Photo by Norma J. Livo.

RACCOONS

The Raccoon and the Redbird
(Native American)

Long ago, when chickens had teeth, a raccoon made some insulting remarks as he passed a wolf. The wolf became angry and turned to chase the raccoon. They both kicked up dust as they ran down a dirt trail; suddenly the raccoon dashed to a tree beside the river. He climbed up with the wolf snarling below him.

The raccoon stretched himself out on a limb overhanging the water. The wolf saw the reflection of the raccoon in the water and, thinking it was really the raccoon, the wolf jumped in the river. He bobbed in the water and nearly drowned before he could scramble ashore. He stretched out on the bank to dry. The warm sun felt so good after the chase and swim and wolf fell asleep.

While the wolf slept, the raccoon came down out of the tree and carefully plastered the wolf's eyes with mud. When the wolf finally woke from his nap, he found he could not open his eyes. The big brave wolf began to cry.

A little brown bird that was passing by heard something he had never heard before—the wolf crying. "What is the matter?" asked the surprised bird.

The wolf whined that he could not open his eyes to see. "If you get my eyes open, I'll show you where you might find some lovely red paint. You could paint yourself all over in red and be like a bright flower among the leaves of the trees. All the other birds would stop where they were and admire your beauty as you sang your sweet songs."

The little brown bird liked this idea and said, "Do you promise not to hurt me if I help you open your eyes?"

"Of course," begged the desperate wolf. "Just help me!"

The bird began to peck at the mud over the wolf's eyes. Ever so carefully and gently the little brown bird worked. It took a long time because the mud had dried and hardened on the wolf's eyes but at last the wolf was able to open his eyes and see again.

Then, just as the wolf had promised, he took the little brown bird to a great rock with streaks of red running through it. Wolf helped the little bird paint each and every feather until he was no longer brown but a gay, happy red.

That is why, to this day, the redbird is this red color. That is also why, to this day, the raccoon still overcomes enemies with cunning.

About the Story

"Raccoon" is an American Indian (Algonquian) name for a small, tree-climbing mammal. Raccoons are mainly nocturnal and are extremely curious. The raccoon is a bright, restless fellow, known for his "bandit's mask," ringed tail, and curiosity. A regular visitor to ponds and streams, the raccoon lives on crayfish, snails, insects, fish, and frogs as well as nuts, fruits, seeds, and eggs. His reputation for washing his meal most likely comes from his habit of feeling his food for texture and size, for the deft animal's acute sense of touch heightens when his fingers are wet.

In northern areas, the raccoon's activity drops off considerably during the winter, but he does not actually hibernate.

The typical raccoon family consists of a mother and her young. In the spring, the female chooses a single mate; she bears two to seven babies nine weeks after conception. Mom becomes teacher, protector, and provider of food. At first she nurses her babies; later she goes in search of solid food to bring back to her young.

Raccoons are born in the spring and are weaned from mother's milk by late summer. Mother shows her children how to climb a tree quickly to escape predators, how to swim, and how to catch mice, frogs, and crickets.

The mischievous raccoon is famous for his nighttime raids on trash cans. Raccoons can find a home almost anywhere, from woodlands to the suburbs. The raccoon's intelligence, agile hands, and liking for a variety of foods ensure his success.

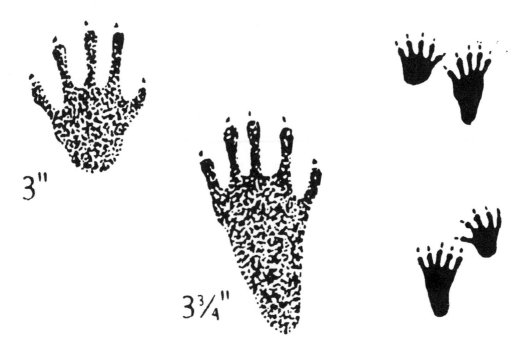

3"

3¾"

Figure 3.5   Racoon tracks.

The raccoon is a gray, nocturnal animal with a black face mask and a bushy, ringed tail. It usually grows to between 16 and 21 inches long with a tail from 8 to 16 inches long. Its weight varies from 12 to 48 pounds. Raccoons inhabit woodlands, riverbanks, and wetlands, but adapt easily to life in the suburbs.

Raccoons are animal tricksters about whom many stories are told in eastern woodlands Native American mythology. In these stories, the raccoon never succumbs to foolishness or allows himself to be tricked.

A television series about Davy Crockett made the raccoon pelt famous as headgear. Davy wore a coonskin hat with the bushy tail hanging from the back. Many youngsters' sole contact with raccoons comes from their Davy Crockett coonskin caps.

Personal Story

During the 1970s, our youngest son, Rob, had a part-time job after school sorting rocks and gravel at a quarry. He and the buddy who also worked at the quarry enjoyed what they were doing; after all, they were paid to play with rocks and dirt in the outdoors.

One evening in the spring, when the trees were just turning green, Rob and his friend were planning to lock up the fenced area they worked in (where they used a conveyor belt) for the weekend. They had heard animal cries from the other side of the lake for a couple of days and decided to investigate before locking up.

They went around the lake to a tall, old cottonwood tree. There, in a hole up in the tree, they found a raccoon's nest with three crying baby raccoons inside. The boys carefully took the baby raccoons out of the nest. They saw several dead babies floating in the lake, who had probably fallen from the tree into the lake. Evidently something had happened to their mother. The boys returned to the quarry, locked up, and came home.

That night, I came home after a night class at the University of Colorado at Denver and there in the front room sat three hulking high schoolers, each holding a baby raccoon and a doll's bottle filled with milk. They were cooing to the babies and coaxing them to drink.

The next day, we took the three babies to the veterinarian. He found them dehydrated and in poor condition and prescribed the proper milk for them; he also advised the boys that the raccoons probably wouldn't survive.

At home again, feeding took place as a regular ritual but, in spite of tender care, two of the babies died. The boys named the survivor "Coonie." Coonie grew and became an interesting family pet—he was housebroken and asked to go outside. I often heard strange noises from inside the cupboard where the cereal was kept: there I would find Coonie, sitting comfortably and helping himself to a box of Cheerios.

Coonie had another habit we laughed at regularly: when we sat on the couch, Coonie climbed up and picked our pockets; he loved that game. He slept on Rob's bed, and when I looked in on them, there was Rob with his head on one pillow and Coonie with his head on the other. Rob laughed about taking Coonie to a local lake to swim; he said that Coonie attracted some neat looking girls.

Coonie and our cat hated each other. We witnessed Coonie's scorn for Mama Cat one day in the recreation room. Coonie and Mama Cat were outside. Coonie grabbed the sliding door and opened it enough to come into the house. Mama Cat was following him but he flipped around, grabbed the door again, and slid it shut in her face.

Our St. Bernard and Coonie were such great buddies that during this time we never needed television; their wrestling and playing was all the entertainment we needed.

One day, Coonie decided to go exploring and went across the backyard into our neighbor's garage. I heard screaming and screeching. When I went to see what was happening, I found the neighbor lady with a broom trying to shoo Coonie out of the garage. Her efforts succeeded only in making the poor animal panic and he hissed and chattered aggressively at her. I picked him up with an apology to the irate broom lady and took him home. Shortly after this, a policeman came to our door and asked if we knew anything about a raccoon. I told him that our son had one as a pet. I couldn't say anything else because there was Coonie right behind me.

The upshot of it all was that we had to build a special cage to specifications to keep Coonie in. We also had to apply for a wild animal refuge permit. When all this was done, an inspector came to check the papers and to examine Coonie in his cage. That was the only time we ever confined Coonie to the cage.

We went for a ride up to the mountains one lovely day and Coonie came with us as usual. We got out to hike and enjoy the mountain top. Coonie scampered up a tree and explored it. We called him when we were ready to go, but Coonie stayed there. To test him, we all got in the car and closed the doors; Coonie scrambled down the tree and ran to the car like a kid that didn't want to be left behind.

Our daughter had her wedding at home and relatives came from everywhere for the event. When we saw the wedding pictures, to our surprise and joy there in the back row was Coonie sitting proudly on Rob's shoulder. Coonie was a true member of the family.

One fall, when Coonie started hiding in the back of Rob's closet, we thought that he might be getting ready to hibernate. Then we noticed that Mama Cat was not her usual active self. We took both Coonie and Mama Cat to the veterinarian and he diagnosed a virus; none of the medication he prescribed worked and within days both Coonie and Mama Cat were dead.

Shortly after Coonie died, we moved the bed in Rob's room; in a corner on the floor we found a collection of Coonie's bright, shiny treasures. Life with Coonie was a joyful learning experience.

FOXES

The Fox and the Horse
(Brothers Grimm)

A peasant had a faithful horse which had grown old and could do no more work, so his master would no longer give him anything to eat and said, "I can certainly make no more use of you, but still I mean well by you. If you prove yourself still strong enough to bring me a lion here, I will maintain you. Now take yourself away out of my stable," and with that he chased the horse into the open country. The horse was mad, and went to the forest to seek a little protection there from the weather.

There a fox met him and said, "Why do you hang your head so, and go about all alone?"

"Alas," replied the horse, "avarice and fidelity do not dwell together in one house. My master has forgotten what services I have performed for him for so many years, and because I can no longer plough well, he will give me no more food, and has driven me out."

"Without giving you a chance?" asked the fox.

"The chance was a bad one. He said if I were still strong enough to bring him a lion, he would keep me, but he well knows that I cannot do that."

The fox said, "I will help you. Just lay yourself down, stretch yourself out, as if you were dead, and do not stir."

The horse did as the fox desired, and the fox went to the lion, who had his den not far off, and said, "A dead horse is lying outside there. Just come with me and you can have a rich meal."

The lion went with him, and when they were both standing by the horse the fox said, "After all it is not very comfortable for you here—I tell you what—I will fasten it to you by the tail, and then you can drag it into your cave, and devour it in peace."

This advice pleased the lion. He lay down and in order that the fox might tie the horse fast to him, he kept quite quiet. But the fox tied the lion's legs together with the horse's tail, and twisted and fastened all so well and so strongly that no amount of flailing could break it.

When he had finished his work, he tapped the horse on the shoulder and said, "Pull, white horse, pull."

Then up sprang the horse at once, and hauled the lion away with him. The lion began to roar so that all the birds in the forest flew out in terror, but the horse let him roar. He drew and dragged him over the country to his master's door.

When the master saw the lion, he was of a better mind, and said to the horse, "You shall stay with me and fare well." Thereafter, the farmer gave the horse plenty to eat until he died.

About the Story

Foxes live in woodlands, hay fields, brushy areas, pastures, and parks throughout the United States. They eat a variety of foods but live mainly on rabbits and voles in winter, shifting to fruits and insects in summer. They are about 2 feet long with a tail from 14 to 17 inches long. They weigh from 8 to 15 pounds. Twenty-one species of fox live throughout the Northern Hemisphere.

Foxes, like cats, have slitted eyes that are well suited for hunting at night. Foxes perform a dance of somersaults and tail chasing to "charm" small animals into sitting still; they have adapted to life in cities and suburbs and have learned to hunt in garbage cans.

The fox is a member of the dog family. Adult pairs mate for life, and both parents put their annual litter of four pups through intensive training in survival skills. The family stays together for an entire summer. Because the life expectancy of the fox is generally only 18 months, only the high birth rate of four pups to each litter allows the species to survive.

Foxes have long illustrated facets of human nature through such myths and legends as "The Fox and the Horse," which characterizes the fox as sly. Fox lore abounds: "To set a fox to keep the geese" refers to an innocent who puts his money into untrustworthy hands. Other cautions include: "The sleeping fox counts hens in his dreams"; "The fox may grow gray but never good"; "The sleepy fox seldom has feathered breakfasts." From the Song of Solomon: "The little foxes that spoil the vines." The Irish name three traits for the fox: a light step, a look to the front, and a glance to each side of the road.

English hunt clubs center on Reynard the Fox. European, Japanese, and Chinese folktales present the fox as a shape-shifter. The fox also appears as a part of the full moon's shifting shape, which in myth is a reversion, a curse, or a form of insanity. Numerous stories tell of fox reward and fox revenge. Legend has it that foxes can make themselves invisible, and can hear everything that is said and read everything that is written. The wise person, therefore, will tell only flattering stories about foxes and keep their wickedness a secret.

In Japanese folklore, the fox is an amazing magical animal capable of bewitching people and assuming human shape. The Japanese consider all foxes malicious. Native Americans tell many stories about Fox as Trickster's companion.

Aesop's many fox fables include "Fox and the Crane," "Fox and the Grapes," and "Fox and the Raven."

Figure 3.7   A fox. Photo by Norma J. Livo.

Personal Story

I enjoy a three-mile walk in a local park situated on both sides of Clear Creek; the wooded areas and lakes provide a rich environment for deer, fox, coyote, skunk, birds, and plants (including a rare orchid).

One fall morning I started my usual walk. I had taken a camera to document a cottonwood tree that had fallen apart but, in spite of holes and a hollow spot in its trunk, still grew some leaves at the top. Because the tree was a study of survival, I took pictures throughout the seasons to document its strong will. I had just taken a picture of the leaves in fall gold when a woman came out of the woods along the path and in a scared voice warned me, "Don't go in there. There could be someone hiding. I think it's dangerous."

It was a foggy morning and the woods did resemble something out of a bewitching fairy tale. I knew every inch of this park, however, and had no fear; I was soon rewarded for that. When I had parked in the parking lot, only one other car was there and I assumed it belonged to the scary and scared lady.

I continued my walk; at one point where the trail ran beside a part of the creek that rushed and splashed over large rocks, a drainage pipe that was under the trail caught my attention.. At the end of the pipe that led out of the woods, I detected a flicker of something furry. I stopped and watched to see what it was. In a humorous scene, a fox backed out of the pipe. When he saw me standing there, he took off at top speed into the woods.

I was smiling as I continued my walk along the trail; when I came to a curve, another fox ran out of the woods to the trail and stopped there; he looked at me eyeball to eyeball. When I stopped walking, he just stood his ground and gave me a steady fox stare. I carefully and slowly lifted my point-and-shoot camera and shot. Naturally, when the camera flashed, so did the fox.

I giggled on the rest of my walk about the scared woman's concern that something dangerous was lurking in the woods. What lurked turned into the great memory of a fox backing out of a drainage pipe and another fox checking me out thoroughly.

Chapter

4

Constellations

"That starred Ethiop queen that strove
To set her beauty's praise above
The sea-nymphs and their powers offended."

Milton, *Il Penseroso*

PERSEID METEORITE SHOWERS

Perseus and Andromeda
(Greek)

In Greek mythology, Cassiopeia, the wife of Cepheus, the King of Ethiopia, was a woman of great beauty. Cassiopeia was the mother of Andromeda.

Unfortunately, Cassiopeia was as proud as she was lovely and made a habit of boasting of her beauty. At first she boasted that she was the most beautiful creature in Ethiopia, then she included the world, and last, she claimed she was the most beautiful either on earth or among the gods.

One day she insulted the water nymphs who lived on the seashore and in the cool waters of bubbling streams. Cassiopeia not only insulted the nymphs but she bragged that she was far more lovely than any nymph who had ever lived. At this, the nymphs complained to their father, Neptune.

Neptune emerged from the sea and plunged his trident deep into the waters. He created a monster unlike any that had ever been known on earth or in the sea. This ferocious and evil creature, Cetus, was sent off to lay waste to the country and strike terror into the hearts of the people.

Cetus performed his assigned job well. Ethiopians fled from the coast in terror and begged King Cepheus to save them. When Cepheus consulted an oracle, he learned that the only way to appease the wrath of Neptune would be to offer his daughter, Andromeda, as a sacrifice to the ferocious, ravenous monster.

Even though the king loved his daughter dearly, he had no choice. And so Andromeda was led to the edge of the sea, chained to a rock, and left there as an offering to Cetus.

During this time, Perseus, the hero son of Zeus and Danae, had been given the almost hopeless task of obtaining the head of Medusa. With the help of the gods, he was successful. Because the head turned all that looked on it to stone, Perseus had to resort to cleverness to slay Medusa and claim the head. He used Minerva's shield, Mercury's winged shoes, and Pluto's helmet of invisibility.

While wearing Mercury's winged shoes, Perseus hovered above Medusa as she slept. He guided himself by the reflection in the shield and cut off Medusa's head; he then flew away across the sea with it. Some drops of blood from Medusa's head fell into the water and Neptune felt these drops. Neptune became overcome with grief because he himself had once loved Medusa.

Neptune lifted up the drops of blood, mixed them with white sand from the beaches and foam from the waves. In this way he created Pegasus, the winged horse.

Perseus mounted Pegasus and flew over the coast of Ethiopia. He saw Andromeda chained to a rock in the sea and used the winged shoes of Mercury to reach her. The rescue wasn't to be without difficulty, though, for Cetus was also approaching the rock, his hungry energy beating up the waters into waves and froth.

Perseus fell upon Cetus and plunged his sword so deeply into the neck of the monster that the blood spouted up and soaked Perseus's winged sandals. They became so wet and heavy that he could no longer fly; he had to balance himself on a rock for the final blow. Perseus then realized what he must do: he held the head of Medusa in front of the monster and Cetus was turned to stone.

Andromeda and Perseus were married and they continue their story as constellations in the sky.

About the Story

All the characters in these adventures became constellations and continued their stories in the sky. Neptune saw to it that the vain Cassiopeia was given a seat in heaven placed so that she would swing completely upside down as she revolved around the Pole Star. There she sits, still in her chair, spending half of every night hanging with her head down. Certainly this position is uncomfortable as well as humiliating.

The constellation of Cassiopeia revolves around the Pole; when it moves below the Pole, it is a slightly distorted capital "M." This reverses when Cassiopeia sits above the Pole, making the constellation a celestial "W."

The Perseid shower, which arrives in mid-August (the best time for stretching out on a high spot and viewing the display of shooting stars), is the most reliable meteor shower each year. Observers can see about 60 flaming meteors an hour, although this number fluctuates.

Observations of the Perseids have been recorded since the tenth century A.D. You need no special equipment to enjoy the show—just get away from city lights. Look to the northeast between 1 A.M. and 5 A.M. for the best viewing.

The shower is named for the constellation Perseus, from which the meteors seem to be falling.

It was during the peak of the Perseid showers one summer that the following story took place. I have never seen a more spectacular sight in the skies since this four-day August trip down the Green and Yampa rivers in Colorado. I have changed names to protect the guilty. Here's the adventure story of a river-raft trip down the Green River—as told by the raft.

Personal Story

They Were All in the Same Boat—Me!

Is anyone sympathetic with synthetics? If so, listen to my tale, because I'm a river raft made of neoprene—fore, midship, and aft. Neoprene, as you know, is synthetic rubber out of which even such necessities as heels and soles of shoes are again being made. Twixt you and me, I carry a lot of good souls (and a few heels) down rivers wild and tame.

I'm described as basic black and silver in color; and I'm 18 feet long and 2 feet deep with a double bladder floor. (Confidentially, I've had my share of bladder trouble.) I am an assault raft, but more assaulted than assaulting. The words "Outward Bound" adorn my sides.

August 12, 1975, while the Perseid meteor shower reached its zenith of 50 observed meteors per hour, seven University of Colorado at Denver faculty persons bedded down in their sleeping bags alongside the Green River on the Gates of Ladore campground. I was also rolled up and I listened to my passengers-to-be as they talked about the meteors radiating from the constellation Perseus. Schiaparelli, the noted Italian astronomer, I learned, back in 1866 determined that Perseus travels the same orbit as Tuttle's comet. Who cares, on a summer night before an exciting river trip?

Morning came sooner than I expected, and those who were to be my crew were up and bustling early. Jerry Dolon (a pseudonym for Joseph Nold, spelled backwards, almost) was their leader. They untied me and unraveled me, then took turns pumping air into my sides, stretching my neoprene to its limits.

Possessions, gear, water carriers, food and bailing buckets (oh, did they even need and really use those buckets?) were stashed within me. Everything seemed shipshape, allowing full freedom for the crew, and they'd use every inch of that space. With all the confusion and rushing around and all, "Where'll we put this?" and "Where'll we put that?", I was glad I was an inanimate object. But that wouldn't last for long. When I think of how animated I was to become—just thinking of it brings an ache from my stem to my stern.

After basic instructions from our Outward Bound river craftsman, Dolon, the crew, all in orange life jackets, thank goodness, scrambled into me and cast off. But, even after the instructions, born of the fantastic experiences of Dolon, I sensed after scanning the crew that my trip down the Green would mean going in circles much of the time. We were off into the mists of adventure. I was boat number two in a flotilla of three.

Commands and confusion intermingled. "Forward paddle!" shouted Dolon. Then "Back paddle!" "Left turn!" "Right turn!" "Draw!" They seemed to come on top of each other and I spun merrily as the creative crew messed up every command. Amidst all this frantic activity, Dolon remained unruffled. But don't conclude that they weren't able to steer me. Once they did . . . it seems. Sometimes, however, I wondered which way was upstream and which way was down. I found some consolation in the sight of the other rafts, caught in the same confusion.

We moored at Winnie's Rapids and I knew that if the trip was a short one, it would seem long to me. I rested while the crew scrambled out of me and hiked up to Winnie's Grotto. I bobbed and tugged at my mooring line and shared my groans with my two companion rafts.

Before I was ready, the disaster group crawled back into me and (bravely?) slammed into almost every sleeper and exposed rock in upper and lower Disaster Falls. It was so bad at one point that the helmsperson ordered the bowperson to land. It was exciting to watch as the noble bowperson, knocked off the perch, disappeared straight down eight feet in the water and then bobbed back to the surface—still clutching the bowline.

A late afternoon rainstorm hit us while we were still out of control, but one charming member said she could cope with wind, rain, and the river. Hail, she said, was another matter, and then the sky opened up with a white, stinging barrage. But she coped. Maybe we were all trying to be as calm and strong as Dolon.

Triplet Falls presented us with our major disaster. I swear the big rock was zooming upstream as fast as we were whizzing down. I held my breath—every puff my crew had pumped into me. Then, wham! My front end wrapped neatly around the upriver side of the inconsiderate rock; my rear half was on the downriver side. The left bowperson spun into the water for an independent float but, in the best river rat tradition, he still clutched his paddle when we picked him up downstream after I was untangled. There's not much neo-persons can do without help in such an ignominious mishap. My patience, deep in my neoprene, was stretched to the splitting point.

Downriver we went, my bottom and sides banging from rock to rock, topping off with a magnificent grand slam into a hard but beautiful cliff below the rapids. My cleverly curious crew tested each rock and found each one as hard as rocks are supposed to be. It was evident my crew was weakening. Their leaps became lunges, their hands became the sprouting beds for blisters. They lost hats and canteens to the boisterous stream, but they shared with each other what they had left.

We all relaxed in lazy stretches of the river and listened to Dolon as he took us poetically into geologic time, telling us when and how stretches of the canyon came into being. He also deftly spun river yarns. I was beginning to like my crew, in spite of everything.

Each night my crew bedded down to watch the Perseid sky show. They "oohed" and "aaahed" in appreciation. On the fourth night, I was treated to a thorough cleaning, after being emptied of what gear hadn't been claimed by the river. I rested contentedly that night, spread on my belly on the sand, listening to the wild cadence of square dance music and the shouts of the spirited dancers. One of my crew had smuggled aboard an autoharp and kazoos. Oh, what I'd do to stretch my neoprene in one of those lively dances and cavort to the tune of "Wildwood Flower," as they did. Then I remembered that I was born to the river where I danced much wilder dances than the crew did on land.

Experience had improved my crew, I had to admit. But, back on the river again, they piled me into another protruding boulder. Boat number three came to my rescue; with a hefty bump we were afloat again.

As we gyrated and bumped our way downstream, I pondered the imponderable, such as the remark made by the big, good-looking fellow, "Colorado stops at no expense." Then the question, "I wonder, how much did it cost to make these canyons? What's the upkeep?"

Mumblings from the sleeping bags puzzled me, too. One crew member said he wanted to go home and be pampered. Another asked, "What's a London city boy doing square dancing in the moonlight in a parking lot in Utah?"

One night, in the middle of meteorite watching, a burst of laughter greeted the declaration of another crew member: "I want you folks to know something. Regardless of what has happened in the past and what will happen in the future, and in spite of all we have been through together, there is one thing I want you all to know—I hate your guts!"

Well, we split at Split Mountain Canyon near Dinosaur Quarry in one final circle that landed me on the ramp. The crew removed my burden, knocked the air out of me, wrapped me carefully, tied me in a bundle, and heaved my 300 pounds of well-beaten neoprene into a waiting truck. How good it will be to ride instead of being ridden, I sighed.

I felt a sudden glow of satisfaction when I looked at that crew. Somehow I had made them look healthier and happier than when, almost with dismay, I first saw them. One of the crew gave me an affectionate pat as I rolled into the truck. I'm sure that even if none had any sympathy for a synthetic, one had a bit of empathy. And that is what I did during the Perseid meteorite showers that summer.

And that is part of the most amazing viewing of the Perseid meteorite showers I have ever experienced. Each summer, in the middle of August, I flee the city lights and hope for more dazzling sky performances, but the night skies are cloudy, or there's a bright moon out, or I fall asleep on the hillside and miss them. Truly, this four days-and-nights raft trip in the pitch-black river canyons was a once-in-a-lifetime front-row seat to a spectacular happening.

"They Were All in the Same Boat—Me!" by Norma J. Livo, *Colorado Outdoors*, March/April 1978, 27–29

ORION

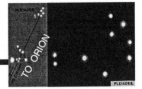

The Orion Constellation
(Greek)

The giant hunter, Orion, was the son of the god Poseidon and of Euryale, the daughter of King Minos and Queen Pasiphae of Crete. Orion experienced many giant-sized adventures. His father had given him the power of wading through the depths of the sea, or, as others say, of walking on its surface. One of his adventures was the result of love. He cleared the island of Chios of wild beasts in return for the hand of his beloved, Merope, the daughter of Oenopion, the island's king.

Orion brought the bodies of the beasts as a present to his beloved, but Oenopion broke his promise of consenting to the marriage no matter what Orion did and how he entreated the king for his daughter. Orion decided to use violence to gain his beloved, and in a drunken rage he ravaged Merope. In revenge, Oenopion blinded Orion and cast him out on the seashore.

Orion waded through the sea and over land toward the home of the god Helios, the sun. Orion was so tall that as he waded in the sea the water came up to his chest. The blinded hero followed the sound of a Cyclops' hammer until he reached Lemnos and came to the forge of Vulcan. Vulcan took pity on Orion and gave him one of his men, Kedalion, to guide him to the home of Helios in the east. Orion carried Kedalion on his shoulders on this trip. When Orion reached Helios, the god restored Orion's sight. Orion did not return to Merope, but instead found favor with several goddesses. He lived with Diana the huntress, but her brother, the god Apollo, was very unhappy about this.

Apollo told the earth goddess Gaia that Orion had boasted that he was the greatest hunter and he could kill every beast in the world. Gaia sent a monstrous scorpion to kill Orion. Orion went off wading through the sea with his head just above the water. Apollo pointed out this "black thing" on the sea to his sister the archer. He taunted her that even with all her skills as an archer she couldn't hit it.

The goddess took careful aim, shot her arrow, and killed Orion with fatal aim. The waves washed the body of Orion to the shore, and when the goddess discovered the identity of the "black thing" she had shot from a distance, she set Orion among the stars as the constellation that bears his name. There he appears as a giant, with a girdle, a sword, a lion's skin, and a club. Sirius, his dog, follows him, and the Pleiads fly before him. And there, in the winter sky, Orion is pursued forever by the scorpion (the constellation Scorpio).

About the Story

Orion travels near the equator. In the winter in the Northern Hemisphere, Orion becomes one of the brightest of the constellations; look for it in the winter skies. The figure of a hunter with a belt and sword represents it on the constellation charts.

Personal Story

Many years ago, while taking a course in children's literature at the University of Pittsburgh, I first heard the story of Orion.

Dr. Miller taught this course; she was lowest on the totem pole in the English department. Dr. Miller thought the course was beneath her and regularly imparted this sentiment to her 70 students. Class consisted of dry lectures and reading assignments from an anthology.

One day, in a tactic that was unheard of for her, she told us the story of Orion. This was a memorable class. It turned out to be memorable in other ways, too.

When it came time for the final test, Dr. Miller instructed the students to write the story of Orion. This obviously was to punish any students who missed her one-of-a-kind telling of this story.

Being a lover of stories, I found this test a pleasure. I quickly wrote the story with all the details she had given us and added some details of my own that I felt belonged in the story to give it more sense.

A week later, a smiling, laughing Dr. Miller came to class clutching our final tests. Never had we seen her so happy; obviously something exceptional had happened.

There we all sat on this last day of class, ready to get our test results and maybe find out what tickled this serious, dour professor. "Class, something has happened that I must share with you," she began. "Someone in the class wrote an outstanding version of the story of Orion. There was only one startling flaw. This person gave the name O'Ryan to the hunter-giant. Isn't that something!" As she said this, she turned to the chalkboard and wrote O'Ryan with an uncharacteristic flourish.

Many in the class gave an uncomfortable laugh, but I just sat there and turned a bright red. That was mine! I knew it because that was how I had spelled Orion. Remember, when she told us the story, I had never seen it in print. I had grown up among a strong Scotch-Irish group of people; how else would you spell O'Ryan?

I have never forgotten that story and the way I felt when Dr. Miller finally found something to enjoy in teaching that class. Orion is one of my favorite bright winter constellations. I have told his story to our four children, our seven grandchildren, and many students. I have also shared my public humiliation concerning my Irish constellation, O'Ryan.

Chapter
5

Plants

"If you always have dry feet, you miss half the fun of life."

Thoreau

COLUMBINE

The Columbine

In pink or purple hues arrayed

Offtimes indeed in white,

We see, within the woodland glade

The Columbine delight;

Some three feet high,

With stem erect,

The plant unaided grows,

And at the summit,

Now deflect,

The strange-formed flower blows.

Anonymous

About the Columbine

The columbine (aquilagia) appears in Chaucer as a symbol of cuckoldry and a deserted lover. It was an insult to give a columbine to a woman and extremely bad luck to give one to a man. The columbine supposedly contained a cure for measles and smallpox; it does contain prussic acid and may have a narcotic effect on some people. Legend has it that lions ate columbines in the spring to gain extra strength.

Among the Native American people of the Missouri River region, Omaha and Ponca bachelors used crushed columbine seeds as a perfume. The Omaha commonly chewed the seeds to a paste, which they spread on their clothes. The Pawnee used the seeds as perfume and a love charm, and women of the Thompson Indian tribe believed the columbine charmed men into giving their affections; the Thompson Native Americans also used the columbine to retain wealth and possessions and considered the flower good luck in gambling.

In 1899, the columbine (see Figure 5.1) became the state flower of Colorado. (At one time there was even an effort to make the columbine the national flower.) Dr. Edwin James, Colorado's first botanist, found the columbine selected for Colorado in 1820. Dr. James, who was also a climber, found the Colorado columbine south of Elephant Rock near Palmer Lake around the first day of July. The enthusiast can follow the columbines in the Rockies from the foothills to the alpine meadows from June to September.

Figure 5.1   Columbines in Colorado. Photo by Norma J. Livo.

"Columbine" derives from the Latin for "dove." The scientific name, *aquilegea coerulea*, comes from the Latin *aquilegea* (for eagle) because the flowers have spurs like an eagle's talons. *Coerulea* means azure, like Colorado's blue sky. When Dr. Edwin James saw blue flowers above timberline on Pike's Peak, he wondered if their proximity to the sky had any relation to their color.

In the Rocky Mountain National Park, columbines have left their names on bays, creeks, falls, and lakes.

Personal Story

As a Pennsylvania native, I revere that state's flower, the trillium. When we moved to Colorado, I had an entirely new passel of state critters and plants to meet; high on my list was the columbine.

Because my mother's talents at growing plants consisted of four-o-clocks, violets, and dandelions, I had not grown up with an appreciation of flowers until I found the trillium; that is when wildflowers became my passion.

I had borrowed my eldest son Eric's 35-millemeter camera for photography needs connected with my classes at the University of Colorado at Denver. (It was easier to give a slide talk on books with selected pictures and passages than it was to lug in bags of books and hold them up in front of the classes.) Another minor detail: when I passed the books around (the discussion at hand never matched the arrival of the corresponding book—there was a time lag, especially for students at the back of the room) and periodically a book never returned. I had done a good job of selling the book but the library and I had a real regular pay-for-the-book tradition.

I also need to add here that I had been content up to this time to let others take the pictures whenever possible. I had absolutely no interest in photography. Others in the family produced the documenting and the artistic pictures.

Back to the camera. My son got tired of me continually using his camera and felt that it was time I bought my own. This I did after some grumbling about ungrateful children. Because I knew all about my son's particular camera, I bought one just like it.

This was in the height of wildflower season in the Rockies and Eric suggested that I buy a supply of slide film and that we go hiking in the mountains and shoot photographs. That way we could compare his camera to mine and make sure that my camera was operating correctly.

We chose to go to Brainerd Lake in the Indian Peaks area and take a trailhead to Lake Isabella for our hike. It was a clear, bright day and we both snapped pictures as we went. We saw many lovely tundra flowers and I got on hands and knees to capture them with the lens. I found plants that I had never seen before; because of the high altitude, many of them were exquisite miniatures. We hiked up steep paths, across snow fields, and through streams with golden marsh flowers growing alongside them.

Then the miracle happened. When we came to Lake Isabella, we rounded a turn in the trail, and there across the corner of the lake in front of me I saw what I had really been looking for—columbines! They were growing out of a flat spot in some huge boulders that overhung the lake. From where I stood, it seemed that the only way I could get a close-up of these, my first columbines, would be to wade into the lake. I did. That water was icy cold. Nothing is colder than water that comes from freshly melting snow.

I carefully made my way to the boulders and took maybe eight shots of the same flowers. I adjusted the meter readings of my camera to make sure I got the perfect picture. This was exciting, if cold, photography.

When I had finished that roll of film, I slogged out of the lake with numb feet and ankles. I sat down on the bank and reloaded my camera. My feet might have been cold but my heart was full of joy.

All through this, Eric, who had gone ahead of me, was laughing. I assumed his laughter was due to my wading in the lake. I finished loading my camera and I got up to go over to tell him about the wonderful discovery I had made. At last I had seen, and now documented on film, the lovely Colorado state flower.

I hurried around another curve in the trail and then I saw Eric and why he was laughing so hard. There, around the bend and behind the boulders I had waded out to, was a glorious patch of blooming columbines. Had I just gone some few yards further around the boulders, I would have saved myself from wet boots and blue jeans for the rest of our hike.

On our return to the city, I took both our films in to be processed; then I got my next surprise. Our son, just in college at that time, had taken pictures of grand vistas and distances. He had shot the pictures of me, too, from a distance. My pictures were all close-ups. The flowers I had shot while on my hands and knees, and even my photos of Eric, turned out almost at nostril distance.

I choose to think that these differences reflected my maturity and ability to appreciate the little things, while his philosophy encompassed the world with his entire future spread before him. It could not have been nearsightedness, I tell myself, because we both wore glasses with corrections for that condition.

What a glorious day it was when I saw my first wild columbines in the mountains, but I have learned a lot more about columbines since then. I know where to go to find patches of columbines in wooded glens and along streams. Although I now grow several varieties in my own garden and have also become a better photographer since that first trip, nothing will match the drama and humor of my first encounter with Colorado columbines.

HACKBERRY TREE

The Legend of Hackberry Hill

On a hill located in a place called Arvada, Colorado, there is a hackberry tree. Naturally the hill is now called Hackberry Hill. However, the tree there now is not the original tree.

When pioneers traveling west came to the Denver area, there was a tree growing on a hill as they headed toward the foothills. One of the earliest records of the sighting of the hackberry tree by white men was made by John Torrey, the naturalist with the 1843 Fremont Expedition.

Colorado plains were generally devoid of trees except for cottonwoods growing in the stream areas, so this hackberry tree served as a landmark for travelers. The tree was also unusual because its territory stopped over 600 miles to the east, near St. Louis. The tree was 14 inches in diameter at its base and was 16 feet high. It had grown in such a manner that its trunk was twisted to form a seat, which travelers used to sit on to rest. The tree bore a reddish cherry-like fruit every year as far back as was known to the white man. How did this tree get where it was?

Some people say this tree, growing all alone on its rocky, barren hill, might have been planted by early explorers. Others suggest that wild birds from the Missouri River Valley carried the seeds to the hill. The Indians, however, had a different idea about the tree's origin.

Native American lore says that all things have a spirit or life force and that all these forces are interconnected. Each animal, each stone, and each place has a unique spirit that influences all life around it. To use medicine is to use the forces of nature to influence and guide one's path in life.

Native Americans wore medicine bags around their necks. When a person assembled a medicine bag, he wished to assert control over his life and to choose a certain path. Each item selected for the bag became a protection charm; the contents of these bags might have included sage, yarrow, and corn (to nourish the spirit), obsidian (for the protection of the ancestors' spirits), and a bear fetish (the bear is the model of the family animal, protecting its young from present dangers). Sometimes items holding special significance for their owners also found their way into the medicine bags.

Long ago, the Native Americans said a great chief killed in battle was buried on the bluff, which was sacred to the Indians. Mountain and plains tribes went to the hill to worship the Great Spirit, hold powwows, and smoke sacred pipes.

The great chief, the Indians said, was dressed in his chief's robes with his favorite war bonnet and healing objects beside him. Around his neck was his medicine bag, which held his personal charms against bad luck. In the bag were hackberry seeds, which were the gift of the medicine man. One of these seeds started to grow within the breast of the chief, sending its branches to the sun and its roots to the water far below.

The Plains Indians, in their old-time burial practices, placed the body upon a scaffold of poles, or a platform among the boughs of a tree; this was their only means of protecting the body from wild beasts, because they had no tools with which to dig a suitable grave. They prepared the body by dressing it in the finest clothes and giving it a secure covering of rawhide. Then the mourners broke camp and departed, leaving the dead alone in an honorable solitude.

However the hackberry tree arrived at its desolate spot, the future was to change things drastically. In 1936, Colorado planned a new road over Hackberry Hill, where the old hackberry tree stood. The engineers decided the tree must be cut down. Many people insisted that the ancient tree ought to be saved, and after much discussion and argument, the officials finally agreed to transplant the tree. They dug a ditch around the tree and carefully left a large mass of soil clinging to the roots. The day before the tree was to be removed, it was mysteriously cut down.

People of the time theorized that the Great Indian Father brought revenge on the white man for building a road that would destroy an Indian altar, but others were more suspicious of the telltale marks of a rusty handsaw on the stump.

Bits of the original hackberry tree remain as mementos. The gavel of the Arvada Garden Club, a group formed in opposition to the destruction of the tree, was made from the old tree.

In 1974, a man named Ford Fox confessed that he had cut down the hackberry tree because he thought too much fuss was being made over the old tree.

In 1966, the Arvada Garden Club planted a commemorative hackberry tree in a small park donated by the Colorado Division of Highways. The plaque reads, "This young hackberry tree was planted here in memory of an old hackberry tree which stood on the top of this hill as a landmark for pioneers coming west. It was the only hackberry tree anywhere around this region for 600 miles" (see Figure 5.2, page 76). The original tree had stood proudly atop the hill with Native Americans, buffalo, and a few white settlers for companions. Its replacement hides in a tiny roadside park beside a heavily traveled, crowded highway. Perhaps the great chief looks down with sadness at the spot where the great hackberry tree, a landmark for weary travelers, long ago sprang from his heart.

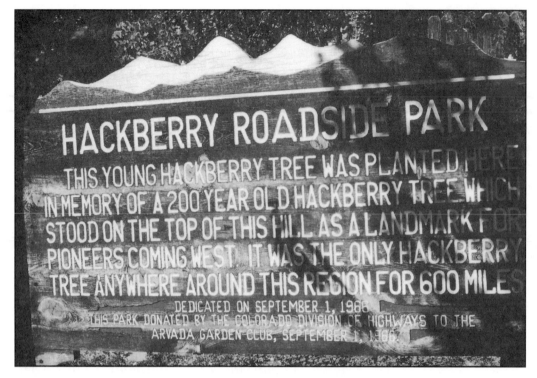

Figure 5.2   The plaque in Hackberry Roadside Park. Photo by Norma J. Livo.

About Trees

Universally, in many religious practices, the tree holds a special meaning. No emblem is more widespread or has exerted greater influence on the institutions of mankind than the tree. The size, strength, and longevity of trees probably impressed the ancients; they also must have been well aware of their own dependence upon the materials and foods that trees produce. For the ancients, trees possessed haunting and magical qualities.

In Scandinavian mythology, Yggdrasil, the world tree, was an evergreen ash whose roots and branches bound together heaven and hell. This cosmic tree, one of the many believed cosmic "world trees," held the universe together. Under Yggdrasil, it was believed, the gods met daily in judgment.

The Christmas tree originated from the pagan practice of worshipping the fir tree during the winter solstice.

Our custom of knocking on wood for good luck also has ancient origins. During the times of the Druids, it was believed that spirits lived in trees; people knocked on trees to announce themselves before they asked the tree spirits to grant their wishes. Woodcutters begged the forgiveness of a tree before they cut it down lest its spirit remain to haunt them.

Many beliefs worldwide concern trees; the following list represents just a sample of these beliefs:

- If, immediately after a storm, you dig at the base of a tree that was struck by lightning, you will find a thunderbolt. Thunderbolts are walnut-sized, look like melted glass, and bring good luck. Dig quickly, or a groundhog will eat the prize before you are able to recover it.

- A tree will grow well, if, when you plant it, you grasp it firmly with two hands, while a second person helps.

- Old trees crashing down in the mountains signal a coming storm.

- A heavy acorn or beechnut crop portends a severe winter.

- A family living nearest to a withered tree will have sickness.

- If you gather some of the fruit from a tree at its very first bearing, and also leave some behind on the branches, the tree will always bear well.

- If you see a few leaves trembling on a tree while the others are still, you will have bad luck.

- If you carve your name into any tree, you will have an enemy that will be with you until the tree is cut down or burned. If you cut your name into a tree, it will die when you die.

- A tree that bears leaves in late autumn foretells many deaths in that vicinity.

- If you come upon a tree standing in the middle of a path, always pass it on the right. To do otherwise is unlucky.

- If the tops of your trees wither, the head of your family will die.

- It is bad luck to cut down a very old tree. The older the tree, the more souls it shelters (Borneo).

- A tree with a trunk that is twisted in the direction of the setting sun will be easily split, but not so the tree whose trunk twists toward the sunrise.

- It is bad luck to pass a place where a tree has been blown down across the road. Remove the tree first.

- If a tree branch grows into your window, you will be successful in achieving those things you wish for.

- If you unexpectedly kill a tree, expect domestic troubles.

- If you are hit by a falling tree, you will not live out the year.

- If you touch a tree that is inhabited by a tree fairy (dryad), the fairy will injure you in some way (Germany).

- If a tree growing near your house splits in two, you will have bad luck, perhaps the death of someone in the family.

- If you cut a tree under a waning moon, the lumber will shrink and decay.

- If you plant a tree that subsequently grows crookedly, there will be a black sheep in the family.

- Never cut, hurt, or disturb a tree that grows near a sacred well (Ireland).

- You will have bad luck if you cut down a green tree.

- If you cut a tender branch from a tree, your children will die young (Persia).

- It is lucky to plant a shade tree (India).

- It is unlucky to sit on a tree stump.

- You will bring poverty if you peel the bark from a tree (Germany).

- If a tree sheds its leaves from the top down in the fall, the winter will be light. Leaves that are shed from the bottom up foretell a hard winter.

- On Orkney, there stood a sacred tree that could not be touched. People believed that even if one leaf were removed, they would be conquered by a foreign nation.

- In the spring, go into the forest and locate a healthy tree. Bite into one of its branches: if that branch later withers and dies, you will also die.

- If you ever cut down a lightning-struck tree, cut three crosses into the stump to keep evil from you.

- You will grow warts if you touch the wart-like growths on a tree.

- The charm of knocking on wood to make a dream or wish come true dates from Druidic times. The Druids believed that gods inhabited trees; to ask a favor of a god, Druids knocked on the trunk of a tree, then waited for a favorable reply—a return knocking.

- In Sweden, a mother who draws her sick child through the exposed roots of a tree will effect a cure for the illness, but only if she does it on a Thursday.

- Burning wood from a lightning-struck tree is bad luck.

- Using a few old pieces of wood to construct a new building is good luck.

- California's Maidu Indians believed that the earth was originally a mass of fire. When the fire collected at the center of the earth, tree roots connected to the fire. Thereafter, the fire could be extracted from the roots of the trees with special drills.

Personal Story

The house I grew up in had three giant buckeye trees in the front. My bedroom (on the second floor) was just a few feet away from its branches. The shadows the trees created at night and the sounds of the wind and rain lashing the tree shaped my imagination. These trees were protectors and their (pre-television) images provided creative entertainment for me.

At the family farm grew a giant, ancient oak tree. Our four children and I spent many hours tramping all over the farm and forests in the vicinity. One day, in the middle of a regular normal area of the woods, we discovered the giant oak tree. On our next trip up to the farm with Dad, we all hiked to the woods to show everyone *the* tree. Seven of us held hands and tried to circle the tree, but it was so big that our hands could not join to make a circle.

Dad was amazed to find this tree because he thought he knew all about the area. This tree suggested to us how forests here might once have looked. Over the years, we shared this tree with friends and family and often made treks to appreciate the tree and to contemplate the events it might have witnessed during its time. On one of our recent trips back to the farm, our children (now leading their own children to the tree) were shocked to see that the old tree was losing branches and showing signs of its coming end. On our last trip to visit it, we found the giant had died. We gathered pieces of the tree to take back to our home in Colorado as a reminder of the joy the magnificent tree had brought to four generations of our family.

A massive oak tree, which had been struck by lightning, also grew on the farm. When my father and my husband cut it down, they discovered a piece of history in the form of a musket ball embedded in the heart of the tree. What had happened? We saved a slice of the tree, counted the rings, and invented scenarios about happenings during its life.

But one tree story, about the pines on Pine Knob, holds special meanings for me. There was a bare knob on the farm, and Dad decided to change its looks. Many times Dad and I climbed to the top of the knob to sit and talk. He told me tales of the days when no planes flew overhead and horses and buggies traveled in swirls of dust on the dirt roads. He showed me the overgrown road he used to take to his grandparents' farm. He told me about the first cars and airplanes and he reminisced about the first plans to travel in space. I also heard many tales about Dad's young daredevil days, when he rode a motorcycle. For me, the knob was a place of stories and memories. In 1948, Dad participated in a reforestation program sponsored by the government; small pine shoots became available through the program, and Dad obtained hundreds of the infant trees.

Our problem was how we were going to plant so many delicate trees as quickly as possible. We needed manpower! I was a student at the University of Pittsburgh at that time and had many friends there; they gladly became part of our manpower solution. We planned a day at the farm to include such events as jumping from the rafters in the barn into mountains of hay; but the main event, of course, was tree planting.

Dad surveyed the knob and placed stakes in the ground to indicate how we would plant circular rows of trees in aesthetic symmetry. We planted one of the larger trees at the peak of the knob to honor my oldest brother David who died in the Korean War. We young folks made short work of planting and carrying water to the tiny trees. That was fifty-one years ago. My friends were rewarded for their work with a great spaghetti-and-meatballs dinner that I cooked on the wood stove.

I have been to Pine Knob many times since the trees were planted (the farm, now a landmark, was named Pine Knob Farm by the locals). On one of our recent trips, our grown children and I stood in awe of Pine Knob. We entered a thick forest of trees, and after a few yards, all sounds from the outside world had disappeared. Absolute silence prevailed. No wind blew. We had stepped from a world swept and scoured by blustery winds into a great, abiding stillness.

We came across a deer resting in the middle of the knob. The creature was surprised to see us, but didn't go crashing out of the woods. It just lay there, secure in our sacred and peaceful pine refuge.

Chapter

6

Creatures from the Water

"There is nothing—absolutely nothing—half so much worth doing as simple messing about in boats."

Kenneth Grahamme

WHALES

Quatie and the Whale
(Makah)

When creatures still interacted with people as equals, a Makah named Quatie heard stories of fish so big that one of them could swallow a whole canoe with a man in it. "I don't believe that this is true," said Quatie. "I will go and find out for myself and then come back and tell you all about it," Quatie told the people gathered in his village at Neah Bay.

Quatie was the size of a ten-year-old boy and was missing one tooth. He sounded funny when he talked because of the missing tooth. His size never held him back, though, and he enjoyed climbing to the top of a far, flat-topped hill.

Every day, Quatie rose early and walked all the way to the top of the hill with only a little package of food to eat. One day, he found a log that was just what he was looking for; with his chisels, he started to shape it into a canoe.

He worked hard each day and returned to his village at night. In the morning he went to the hill again. He worked on the canoe until the sides were as thin as the length of his little finger. When the canoe was as light as he could make it, Quatie asked eight friends to go with him to the top of the hill and help carry the canoe to the river. The canoe was well-balanced and sailed easily. Quatie and his friends floated the canoe down to a good spot on the shore, where Quatie finished making it.

When his canoe was finally finished, Quatie went to the beach where the large mussels grew and gathered up as many of the mussel shells as his canoe could carry. Then he scraped the shells against stones to make them very, very sharp.

When he had piled his canoe high with sharpened mussel shells, Quatie paddled it over to Tatoosh Island. He climbed out onto the beach and stood there with his arms stretched out to the ocean and chanted a song: "Here I am. I will paddle my canoe on your waters. Send me your worst!"

Early the next morning, he paddled off in his canoe. He had paddled quite some time when a huge fish swam up. Just as the old stories had told, the fish swallowed Quatie and his canoe in one big gulp.

Inside the great fish, Quatie picked up a sharp mussel shell and started cutting the fish. He cut and cut the insides of the fish so that it would be forced to swim toward the beach. For days he cut the insides of the fish with shell after shell. Finally, the huge fish beached itself on the shore.

Quatie quickly ran out of the great fish's mouth and ran all the way to his village. "Come, come!" he called. "Everyone come to the beach. You will find a big fish there. There will be enough food for everyone. Come, hurry, come!"

The entire village ate and held a potlatch to insure that history would be recorded and that Quatie would be remembered for proving the old story true and for giving a gift of food to the tribal members.

About the Story

The Makah Indian Nation lives along the northwest coast of the Olympic Peninsula in Washington state. The culture is traditional and stories and artifacts have preserved a record of life before Europeans arrived. In 1969, the remains of an ancient Makah village was discovered at Ozette. Artifacts of wood, bone, and stone dated back to the early fifteenth century.

The Makah were self-sufficient, although they traded with distant tribes. The Makah wore clothes made of cedar bark along with other fibers, fur, and duck down. They used canoes to go whale hunting.

The story of Quatie is recorded in baskets (see Figure 6.1) the women at Neah Bay craft from wrapped-twine cedar strips. The Pacific Northwest Native American myths, rich in symbolism, are a reminder of a mythic past and a way to communicate with the supernatural world.

Figure 6.1   Basket (crafted by Makah elder Isabel Ides) illustrating the legend of "Quatie and the Whale." Photo by Colorado Camera of Lakewood.

About Whales

The biggest animals on earth live in the sea, not on land. Whales are mammals of the sea. The gray whale, which was probably what Quatie hunted, is 55 feet long and weighs 30 tons. These whales, whose migration is longer than that of any other mammal, make a 10,000-mile round-trip each year. They travel up and down the Pacific coast of North America from the Arctic waters of the Bering Sea to protected lagoons of Baja California, Mexico.

People have been hunting whales for at least a thousand years. At first, whalers hunted from land by watching for the blowing whales; then they set out in small boats. Sometimes, whale hunters drove the whales ashore. Sometimes they speared whales with harpoons and towed them ashore. Over time, bigger ships sailed into deeper waters to hunt.

Whales provided food, oil, and baleen (whale bone). In recent years, scientists raised an alarm about the dwindling numbers of whales, and in 1986 most whaling countries agreed to stop or to severely reduce hunting. In 1997, supported by President Clinton's administration and a $310,000 grant from the Commerce Department, the Makah won an exemption from the worldwide whaling ban and has the right to take up to five gray whales per year for five years. The tribe feels a deep spiritual need to continue hunting the gray whale.

Personal Story

In the 1980s, I was teaching summer classes on storytelling at Leslie College in Cambridge, Massachusetts. One day another professor and I decided to rent a car and drive up the Atlantic coast on a serendipity trip.

We stopped at various fishing villages and places of historical interest, and climbed mountains overlooking bays. Our visit to Rockford was magical, though. Bettie and I found a bed-and-breakfast called The Captain's, located on the rocky shore. Our rooms on the second floor overlooked the sea.

We bought tickets for a boat trip around the area. When the captain told us that he had recently seen whales in the channel between the shore and an island, we (neither of us had ever seen a whale in its natural world) started to fantasize about whales.

Then it happened—a whale appeared on the right side of the boat and blew air from its blowhole; it then arched its back and dived beneath the water. To our amazement and delight, this whale played with our boat and put on an amusing show; for an hour, the creature surfaced and dived and blew bubbles all around us.

After the boat trip, we returned to our bed-and-breakfast and sat on some rocks to gaze out at the channel. There, to our joy, we could see the our whale playing; it was almost as if it knew that Bettie and I were a fascinated audience.

We went into the village and bought some crackers, cheese, wine, and fruit and took the feast back to our rocky theater-by-the-sea seats. We sat there past dusk, all the while glimpsing our magical show. That night, I opened my window and I am convinced I could hear our whale friend playing in the dark.

The rest of the trip was beautiful, but we had received our special treat. When we returned to the campus, we bragged to everyone who would listen about our experience. Many of our professional cohorts looked at us with envy and quietly told us that we had seen something they had never seen, even though they lived in the area. When I think of this experience, I whisper "thank you" to our special nomad of the sea.

FISH

The Magic Fish
(Finland)

There was once, I don't know where, beyond seven times seven countries, and at a cock's crow even beyond them, an immense, tall, quivering birch tree. This birch tree grew long, seven times seventy-seven branches. On each branch there were seven times seventy-seven crow's nests, and in each nest, seven times seventy-seven young crows. It was in such a place that this story belongs.

There was once an old fisherman and his wife who lived by the shore of a clear blue lake in a small house made of logs. The fisherman had fished in the nearby lakes for more than seven times seven years. The fisherman's wife grew flax and wove cloth from the flax. She also raised some sheep for their wool. Between the two of them, they ate well and were warmly dressed, and that was that.

One morning, the fishing was very poor. The old fisherman had caught nothing, but he decided to cast out his net one more time. This time when he gathered in his net, he had one fish. Not just an ordinary fish, but one that was made of pure gold. Its fins were gold, its scales, eyes, and tail were gold.

"Ah, well, this special fish is better than nothing," he said to himself, and opened his birch bark fish basket to put the gold fish in for the trip back home. "My wife will find pleasure in this beautiful fish."

Just as he started to drop the gold fish into his basket, it began to implore him, "Put me back into the lake, old fisherman. If you do, I'll give you whatever you ask me! I'll reward you richly."

The old fisherman stroked his gray beard, and being a kind, gentle man, he carefully slid the fish back into the lake. "Enjoy, little fish. Go back where you belong."

When he returned home, his wife took his fish basket and looked in to see what he had caught that day. There was nothing in the basket. "How can this be? There are no fish for supper in here!" she grumbled.

"I was able to catch only one fish today, but it was a special one. It was pure gold and it talked. It promised to reward me richly if I returned it to the lake, so I took pity on it and let it swim free," he told her.

"What? You mean that you let such a wonderful fish escape? Why didn't you ask it for a house that has a roof without leaks?" she scolded him.

The fisherman didn't like it when his wife was cross with him, so he went back to the shore of the lake. "Golden fish, golden fish," he called out.

He saw the fish swim right up to the beach in front of him. "Why did you call me?" asked the fish.

"My wife wants a house that has a roof without leaks," explained the old fisherman. "Can you help us?"

"Go home. It is done," said the fish before it turned and disappeared into the lake.

When the fisherman got back home, lo and behold! Their log house had a new roof with sturdy beams and thick thatch on it.

Instead of being pleased, his wife scolded him even louder. "If the fish can do this, why don't you ask it for a fine new house with a separate room to sleep in?"

The old fisherman knew there would be no peace that night unless he did as she asked. He went back to the lake and called, "Golden fish, golden fish, I need you."

Just as before, the fish swam into the shallow water near the old man's feet. "You have called me. What do you want from me?" asked the fish.

"Forgive me, you amazing fish. I thank you for the new roof on our cabin, but now my wife wants a fine new house with a separate room to sleep in," the old man told him.

"Go home. It is done," said the fish and it turned, flipped its tail, and was off into the lake.

When he went back home he wasn't sure if he had taken a wrong turn, because where his log cabin used to be sat a beautiful red-painted house, with shutters, a porch, and curtains. Inside was a big kitchen with a large fireplace with a big chimney that had room in the back of it for a person to rest and get warm. There were fine curtains, rugs, and just as he had asked, a separate room to sleep in.

But his wife still wasn't satisfied. "You have no imagination, husband!" she shouted at him. "Why didn't you ask the fish for a castle. I don't want to be a peasant all my life! I want to be a fine lady with fancy clothes and jewelry. Why shouldn't we have a carriage with horses, too? I'm furious that you didn't think of asking for this." She threw a plate at him for emphasis. Luckily, he ducked and the plate smashed into the wall of the new house and flew into many pieces.

So, back to the shore of the lake he went. Would his wife never be happy? "Golden fish, golden fish, I really need your help."

With a ripple and a splash, the fish swam to the shore. "What is it old fisherman? Why do you call me?"

The old man explained. "Please excuse me, dear fish, but my wife is crankier than I have ever seen her. She even threw a dish at me. Please excuse me, but I do need your help. Now she wants a castle, fine clothes, jewelry, a carriage, and horses. What am I to do?"

"Go home. It is all as you have asked," announced the fish as it jumped back into the lake.

Sure enough, when the old man got back to where his cabin had first been, then the house that replaced it, he found a fancy castle with several stories. He could see special places on the upper-story outside walls where he and his wife could have their own indoor facilities for toilet needs. He found his wife inside the castle sitting at a long carved wooden table in an elaborate padded chair carved with the faces of animals.

"I hope that you are happy now," he said. "What more could people such as us want?" He was sure that this was all that anyone could want. The windows even had glass in them to let in the light yet keep out the winds. The golden fish had given them riches beyond dreams.

Weeks went by, and his wife tried on all her new clothes, went for rides in her carriage, and grew more and more impatient. Then, as if she could hold it no longer, she exploded. "Is this the best that the fish can give us? As I ride around I see other people with great armies. I want bands that will constantly play music for us. I want stables of horses. I want the finest amber jewelry that there is. I want grand boats that travel around the lakes so that everyone can see that I am of highest royalty. I want bands to play music on the boats so that everyone can hear our joyous travel up and down the lakes." Her shrill shrieks could be heard throughout the castle.

As the old man walked back to the shore of the lake he wondered how it all could have come to this. Was there no pleasing her? Where would her greed get them? But wearily he called out, "Golden fish, golden fish. Do not be angry, but my wife has sent me back to ask for yet more."

With a swish and a splash the fish appeared. "What is it this time, old man? What more could this wife of yours want?"

The old fisherman told the fish the latest demands. The fish stood on its tail, twirled around, and said, "Go home, it is done," as it dashed back into the lake.

Sure enough, before he even got home, he saw a huge boat loaded with people having a party out on the lake. A band played music on the boat. There was more. The old man had to make his way through enormous armies to get into the castle. There sat his wife, listening to a band playing marches and dance music. She was covered with amber necklaces, bracelets, rings, and earrings and had amber beads hanging from her gown. Truly the fish had done all that was asked and more.

But again, this wasn't to be the end of it. His wife threw golden goblets at him and demanded that she become the mighty ruler of the lakes and rule over the golden fish. She wanted her castle to sit in the middle of the lake, rising to the sky. She demanded the power to raise storms that would strike terror into the hearts of people and beasts that beheld it. "You go tell the golden fish what I want!" she screamed. She was so furious that he did not dare to refuse her wishes.

At the shore, the trembling old fisherman became aware of a great storm raging in the lake. Waters billowed and roiled over the shore. Clouds burst forth walls of water. But still he called out, "Golden fish, golden fish. Hear my cry for help!"

Out of the storm appeared the golden fish. This time the fish was clearly an-gry. "What more could this woman possible want? Has she no shame? What is it this time?"

The soggy, beaten old fisherman told the golden fish of his wife's new de-mands. "Forgive me, golden fish . . ." he said as he bowed his head.

Before the old man could finish what he was saying, the golden fish turned around and slapped his tail on the water and slid back out into the deep.

When the old fisherman returned home, there was his old log cabin with the roof that leaked. On the doorstep sat his old wife dressed in her old patched and tattered clothes!

Adapted from *The Enchanted Wood and Other Tales from Finland* by Norma J. Livo and George O. Livo (Englewood, Colo.: Libraries Unlimited, 1999), 96–100.

About the Story

Many ancient religions associated fish with love goddesses and the fertility of nature; but at the same time the fish is "cold blooded" and therefore considered to lack the heat of passion.

Today the fish (from the Greek, *ichthys*) as a symbol is understood to stand for Greek ("Jesus Christ, Son of God Savior"). The fish became a secret symbol by which persecuted early Christians recognized each other. Some believe that im-mersion in the baptismal font (literally "fish pond") and the reference to the Apos-tles as "fishers of men" were also sources of fish symbolism. The fish was considered a symbol of good luck.

In ancient Egypt, the common people ate fish, but not ordained priests and kings because fish were associated with negative myths.

The eel and perch were considered divine and sacred. Legends of monstrous fish in old bestiaries show both the fascination and fear of these silent inhabitants of the deep. Hindu myth has the god Vishnu taking the form of a fish to save the ancestral father of the human race, Manu. The Chinese saw the fish as a symbol of happiness and plenty. In Japan, the carp stands for courage, strength, and endur-ance because it can make its way through eddies and waterfalls. The Japanese celebrate May 5 by placing banners decorated with pictures of carp in front of their houses.

Pisces, the sign of the fish, is the last sign of the zodiac; those born under Pisces strive for perfection and work cheerfully.

According to the Bible, Christ fed a multitude with only two fishes and five loaves. The Pope wears a fisherman's signet ring signifying Peter's miraculous "draught of fishes."

The Carib believe that fish are always young and that men who lived on fish never grew old. In an ancient Chinese version of Cinderella, a fish instead of a fairy godmother helps the heroine. In Greenland, eating a certain fish was thought to have made women, and even men, pregnant.

Personal Story

Soon after George and I married, we went up to northern Canada to visit George's parents, who lived on the Winnipeg River in the Lake of the Woods country. One day, George and I, along with George's parents and his sister, loaded up the family canoe (22 feet long) and took off for a fishing and camping trip.

I was raised on the Allegheny River in western Pennsylvania when the river was tragically polluted. Steel mills dumped their toxic waste right into a four-mile stretch of the river, as did the aluminum plant, the glass plant, and some coal mines. Because local towns dumped raw sewage directly into the river, we often saw "little brown logs" (as we called them) floating by.

My brothers and I used the river in a variety of ways. My brothers built a boat they named the "sieve," because it was. We would paddle out in it to catch the waves from paddlewheel barges going up and down the river. We fished and reeled in ugly mutations of fish that could have modeled as characters in a science fiction story; we even swam. It is a wonder that we survived our joyous moments in this beautiful but heavily polluted river.

And now here I was, in a stable boat on a river that was so clean you could drink directly from it. The fish we caught were beautiful, unblemished, and edible.

At one point in the trip, we stopped on a large island to fish, make coffee, and have lunch. The coffee bubbled in a granite pot and George's mother and I made the sandwiches. George's sister, Leona, fished idly from the shore.

Suddenly, Leona screamed. She had a fish on her line. She had a *big* fish on her line. We all rushed over to watch the contest; the fish was clearly winning because it took off with Leona's rod and reel. Now George was not about to let a fish do that, so, along with his coat, shoes, and watch, he jumped into the water. We watched him wrestling something big. They splashed and struggled until, victoriously, George waded ashore hugging the biggest fish I had ever seen. It looked like something out of Jonah and the Whale.

The fish was five feet long, a monster muskellunge. Never before had I seen a muskellunge or even been aware that such a fish existed. The Allegheny River and its gross mutants had not prepared me for this!

Later, Mom baked the fish and it tasted wonderful. From that day forth, legends had more meaning for me. I had seen two legends that day: a husband who wore bruises to attest to his struggle, and a fish resembling something from ancient folklore.

Chapter

7

Natural Phenomena

"My hunch is that the sense of wonder is fragile; once crushed, it rarely blossoms again but is replaced by varying shades of cynicism and disappointment in the world."

Rachel Carson in *A Sense of Wonder*

FLOODS

Flood: Creation Story
(Hmong)

A very long time ago, the universe turned upside down. The earth tipped up, the sky rolled over, and the whole world was flooded with water. All living beings were killed, except one brother and his sister, who had run and taken refuge in an unusually large wooden funeral drum. There were no fathers, no mothers, no babies, no chickens, no pigs, no oxen, no buffaloes, no horses, no insects, no squirrels, no rats, no worms, no ants, and no birds left in the world. Only the brother and his sister.

The water rose higher and higher until it reached the sky. Then the drum they were hiding in bumped against the land of the sky and made a sound like NDOO NDONG! NDOO NDONG!

Sky world heard the sound and the ruler of the sky people said, "Go and visit the earthly world to see why it's making this noise. What could be happening?"

Sky people were sent down and they saw that the water had already covered the earth and had reached up as high as the sky. The sky people said, "Let us use copper lances and iron spears to puncture holes in the earth so that the water can flow away."

The sky people hurled their lances and spears into the earth, poking holes, and the water flowed down and away. The big drum floated until at last it came back to the surface of the earth. When the brother and sister heard the drum bumping on the earth, they broke it open and climbed out.

"Where are all the people?" the girl asked.

"Dead," said the boy.

"Are all the animals dead, too?"

"Yes, there is only you and me."

They were both filled with despair. For many months the boy kept asking the girl to marry him so they could have children. She would not listen to him, but his persistence in asking gave her an idea as to how he could stop it once and for all. "Well, if you really want to marry me, we must each take a stone up to the top of that mountain. When we get there, we will roll each stone down different sides of the mountain. The next morning, if both stones have gone back up the mountain and we find them lying together on the mountain top, then I will marry you. I don't think they will come back up the mountain. If they don't, you must stop asking me to marry you."

They took two stones that were used for grinding and that fit together smoothly far up to the top of the mountain. The sister rolled her stone down one side while her brother rolled his stone down the other.

That night, the boy went to the mountain in the dark. He really wanted to marry his sister very much. He found his stone and carried it up the mountain and put in on the grass. Then he went down the mountain and found his sister's stone. He carried it back up to the mountain top.

In the morning the sister said, "It is too bad there was no one to come along with us as a witness." The two of them went back up to the top of the mountain.

"Look at the stones!" said the brother. "They have come back up the mountain and are together in the same place. This is a sign that we can be married."

Finally she agreed; after all, the sign said that it would be all right. They married and lived together as husband and wife. After a while, they had a baby but it was not like just any ordinary baby. Theirs was round like a stone, a soft stone with no arms and no legs. "What kind of a baby is this?" the wife asked.

"Maybe it is a baby seed. Let's cut it into pieces." her husband replied.

They cut the round baby seed into little pieces and threw them in all directions. Some pieces fell into the garden and made people. Their name was Vang because Vang sounds like "garden" in Hmong. Some pieces fell in the weeds and grass and made more people. Their name was Thao because Thao sounded like "weeds and grass" in Hmong. Some pieces fell on the goat house; the people from those pieces were called Li. Li sounded like "goat house" in Hmong. Other pieces fell in the pig house and those people were named Moua. Moua sounded like "pig house" in Hmong.

Vang, Thao, Li, and Moua are some of the Hmong clan names. Three days later, the village was full of houses for every family. People were making fires and smoke was curling through every roof.

But this wonderful seed child of theirs had not been born to create only people. Pieces of it also made chickens, pigs, oxen, buffaloes, horses, all sorts of insects, rodents, and birds. This is how the world was once again filled with living creatures.

The brother and sister said, "Now we aren't sad anymore because we are not alone now."

Chippewa Flood Story
(Chippewa)

According to Chippewa legend, the flood was a result of the melting snow. In the beginning of time, in the month of September, there was a great snow. The snow blew down in a blizzard and swirled around day after day.

A little mouse nibbled a hole in the leather bag that contained the sun's heat, and the heat poured out over the earth. It was so intense that it melted all the snow in a short time.

The melted snow water rose to the tops of the highest pines and kept on rising until even the highest mountains were submerged. One old man had foreseen the flood and warned his family and friends, but they just replied, "When it comes, we'll take to the hills."

They were all drowned, however. Only the old man was left because he had built a large canoe in which he drifted on the flood waters, rescuing whatever animals he encountered.

After a while, he sent out the beaver, the otter, the muskrat, and the duck in turn to try to find land. Only the duck returned, bringing mud on its bill. The old man cast the mud on the waters and blew on it and it expanded into an island large enough to hold him and all the animals. That is how the world began again after the great flood.

The Flood
(Apache)

A long time ago when the earth was younger than it is today, the clouds became thick and dark and filled with rain. Raindrops struck the earth and spattered in miniature explosions of moisture. The rain fell and fell and fell and fell. The waters rose in the streams and became raging rivers. The plains were covered with water and still the waters rose.

As the rain fell and the waters rose higher and higher, the great chief led his warriors higher and higher into the Superstition Mountains. The higher they climbed, the closer the waters came. When the chief realized that even the highest peaks would be submerged, the chief chanted and sang and turned his braves into stone statues rather than let them drown ignominiously.

If you travel to the Superstition Mountains in Arizona, look up high and you will see them standing today, guarding the heights.

Noah and the Flood
(Genesis 6–9)

There was a great wickedness among the people on earth. There was corruption and violence everywhere and the Lord said, "I will destroy mankind." He spared Noah because Noah had found grace in His eyes.

The Lord told Noah to make an ark of gopher wood with rooms in it. He told him to seal the ark inside and outside with pitch. The ark was to be built three hundred cubits in length and fifty cubits in breadth. The height was to be thirty cubits. He also told Noah to build a window and a door in the side of the ark. It was to be three stories high.

The Lord told Noah that there would be a flood upon the earth that would destroy all flesh and everything would die. He instructed Noah to take his three sons, Shem, Ham, and Japheth and their wives along with Noah's wife into the ark. Noah was to also bring two of every sort of animal, male and female, onto the ark. There were fowls, cattle, every creeping thing of the earth.

Noah gathered all the food that would be needed to eat to keep them alive. They went in two by two into the ark as the Lord commanded them.

It rained for seven days and seven nights and the waters of the flood were upon the earth. The windows of heaven were opened and it rained for forty days and forty nights. The water rose and covered all the high hills. All the mountains were covered and all flesh died that moved upon the earth except for those safely floating in the ark. The waters flooded the earth for a hundred and fifty days.

The Lord made a wind to pass over the earth and the waters receded. After seventeen months, on the seventeenth day of the month, the ark came to rest on the mountains of Ararat. After ten months the tops of the mountains were seen.

Noah opened the window of the ark and sent a raven out to see if the waters were dried up from the earth. He also sent a dove but the dove found no rest for her feet and she returned to the ark. Noah waited another seven days and again sent the dove out. This time it did not return to the ark. Noah then removed the covering of the ark and saw the dry ground.

The Lord blessed Noah and his family and instructed them to be fruitful and multiply and replenish the earth.

About These Stories

Since the dawn of civilization, people everywhere have created legends about monstrous floods that ravaged the entire face of the earth. Scholars believe the Hebrew narrators of Genesis borrowed the flood story from the ancient Babylonians.

A Norse myth tells of a worldwide flood brought about by the gushing blood of an evil god who had been slain by Odin and his two brothers. Aristotle, the Greek philosopher, accepted as fact the story of how Prometheus saved people from extinction by warning his son Deucalion of a calamitous global flood.

Lithuanian lore tells of a god named Pramzinas, who created the great flood and then sat eating nuts while peering down to inspect the damage. He dropped one of the celestial nutshells onto a mountaintop providing a vessel for a few survivors to float in until the waters receded.

Native Americans of North and South America tell many stories of a great flood. Consider the long bitter winters of Minnesota and North Dakota, which are often followed by damaging spring thaws. The Mandan Indians believed that soon after the Mandan tribe came upon the earth, a great flood arose and would have destroyed them had not a wise Mandan, the First Man, built a great canoe and hurried the people into it. The sturdy canoe weathered the fury of the waters and finally came to rest on a high hill near the Cannonball River, North Dakota. In Mandan villages, the lodges always faced a large barrel or hogshead, called the Big Canoe, which stood as a symbol for the canoe that saved the Mandans.

For us, frail mortals struggling for survival amid the ravaging waters of a great flood, it may indeed have appeared that the entire world was stricken. Flood plains have always held an irresistible attraction for human beings. Because we have long depended on rivers as arteries for commerce and communication, we have always built towns and cities in flood plains. To repeat, floods are a common natural phenomenon.

Personal Story

I was six years old and it was March in western Pennsylvania. It had been a hard, cold winter, but March had blown in like a lamb and warmed things up. We lived four blocks above the Allegheny River, which was controlled by dams and locks for river travel.

On March 17, Saint Patrick's Day, the frozen ice on the dam and river burst open and the pent up water flooded our town of Tarentum. The water rose quickly and everyone abandoned the town for higher ground. The firemen evacuated people with boats.

From our window on the first floor, I could see that the house below ours had water up to the second floor. Our house was on a knoll; when the firemen came to get us, we left through the front room window. My two older brothers, my mother, and I were going to stay with Grandmother. Dad was staying behind because he was the chief engineer of the municipal electric plant.

We had to leave as quickly as we could with no luggage, so I was fashionably dressed in layers; I felt as if I were wearing every piece of clothing I owned. In all those pants, dresses, sweaters, and a coat, I looked like a clown waddling around.

Dad set up housekeeping in the attic. He had rescued my brother's rabbits from their pen under the back porch and taken them to the attic, too.

When the flood waters receded, we returned home. What a mess: mud and more mud everywhere. At that time a government-sponsored group called Works Progress Association (WPA) employed people because the Great Depression was still holding the country in its grip. (We sometimes referred to the WPA as "We Poke Along" because the workers seemed to lack energy.)

Some WPA workers helped clean people's houses. Dad said we had some especially good WPA workers because they cleaned parts of our car in the garage, too—things just disappeared.

The attic was a mess, too. The rabbits, Snowball and Peter, had chewed and wreaked havoc throughout; but their attic damage did not represent the best of what those rabbits did.

As the mud settled, the real proof of their prodigious efforts became apparent: the entire back yard had sunk! Normally the rabbits were penned up under the back porch, but they had quietly burrowed throughout the yard to pass their time. When things settled after the flood, the yard caved in on their burrows.

Floods did a lot of damage to our town that year, but in spite of it all, we were luckier than most.

Compare flood stories with others, for example, this folktale from Peru: *Llama and the Great Flood* by Ellen Alexander (New York: Crowell, 1989).

LIGHTNING

The Damaged Sun Dial
(based on a true story)

This true story was told me on September 6, 1989. The names have been changed.

Emily's husband had lost his fortune in the oil and energy crash in the 1980s in Colorado. Emily and her husband, Brett, had to sell their magnificent custom-built home in the mountains and move to more modest quarters. Brett had managed to avoid filing for bankruptcy by meeting the monthly loan payments. There was no money left over after meeting the required payments, but it meant a lot to him to meet his obligations honorably.

Emily, a middle-aged woman, no longer lived a life of leisure. She took a job to help make ends meet. Brett and Emily's lives had changed drastically. But worse was ahead.

One day, a business associate, from whom Brett had borrowed money, called him and demanded a meeting. At the meeting, the associate insisted that Brett pay off the entire loan immediately because he feared Brett would file for bankruptcy. Brett assured his associate that he would continue to meet his obligations and that he would never default. As they talked, the associate opened his desk drawer, took out a pistol, cocked it, and placed it hard against Brett's temple. "Give me my money or you die!"

Brett repeated he could not give him all the money but that he would meet each month's responsibility promptly. They discussed and argued for three hours; the entire time the gun was pressed to Brett's head. Finally, the businessman lowered the gun and said, "If you fail to meet a payment, I will kill first your wife and then one by one your children."

As soon as Brett left the office he contacted the local police to report the threat. The police verified that the mark from the pressure of the pistol on Brett's temple was visible. Charges were filed against the businessman and he was ordered to stay away from Brett, Emily, their family, and their home.

Emily began to have night terrors and nightmares, including the scene with the gun pressed to Brett's head; in her nightmares, Emily was a witness, and screamed desperately in her sleep. Brett found it hard to wake Emily up when she screamed in her sleep. One day, her blood pressure shot up dangerously.

When medication didn't control the blood pressure, Emily's doctor tried new remedies. He finally suggested that Emily go to see a psychotherapist who specialized in biofeedback treatment of high blood pressure. The psychotherapist was Dr. Susan Lighter. The treatments she prescribed for Emily began to have a positive effect. As the treatment continued, Dr. Lighter asked Emily to describe her dreams. The two became friends.

During one visit, Emily described a particularly strange dream: "You'll never believe the dream I had last night! In my dream I had driven to the mountains and the dirt road passed under an arch with the town of Sugar Loaf named on it. I parked my car at a trailhead and climbed the mountains. A severe lightning storm broke out. I had climbed past the tree line and knew I had to get down out of there fast. As I rushed past huge boulders, the electricity from them snapped and crackled my wool poncho. Then the storm was directly overhead and I had no choice but to stoop down beside a large rock, being careful not to touch it. I crouched down and covered my head to be as low and become as small as I could.

Then, lightning struck the rock beside me and split it. As I looked up in wonder that I was still alive, a woman in a four-poster bed, which was hanging from chains attached to beams, floated near me. The woman sat up in the bed and said, 'What do I have to do to get your attention? I want my sun dial back!' "

The blood drained from Susan's face and she became so quiet that Emily couldn't even see or hear her breathing. Susan stood up, pushed her chair back and said, "Excuse me. I need to be alone for a while." With that she left the room.

Emily sat there, stunned. What had happened? Susan had looked so pale that Emily began to think she might be sick. After a short while, fearing that Susan might need help, Emily followed her. When she found Susan, she asked, "Are you sick? Can I do something to help you? Can I get something for you?"

Susan stared at her with a shocked look. "Let's go back to the office. We'll talk there."

Once again, seated in the office, Susan started: "I feel I need to tell you a story. I had a very special friend, Della Mae, who lived in a log cabin in Sugar Loaf. During the 1970s, transients and hippies roamed and squatted in old cabins, caves, and abandoned mines in many of Colorado's small mountain towns. One night, one of them broke into the cabin of an old fellow and beat him brutally. The old man, a widower, was left in a crumpled heap on his kitchen floor. The attacker calmly cooked himself a meal and ate it at the table. Then he kicked the old man one more time, ransacked the cabin, and left.

Della Mae found the old man still there on the floor when she came by to check on him. She hadn't seen him for two days and was worried. The poor fellow was hospitalized for two weeks, but he recovered enough to return to his cabin. While he had been in the hospital, neighbors had cleaned his home and repaired the damaged furniture. The old man seemed to feel better at home, but tightly secured his place. He even adopted a German shepherd puppy for company as well as for an alarm signal and protection.

One late afternoon, Della Mae brought the man a meal she had prepared for him. She called to him from the yard as she walked to the door. There was no answer. Then, she knocked on the door. The old man had lost his hearing from the beating and did not hear her calls. Shots rang out. Bullets splintered the door and killed Della Mae."

Susan paused and continued as she took a deep breath: "I was living in Michigan when this happened, and got the telephone call telling me about Della Mae's death while I was in bed. My bed was a four-poster and hung by chains from beams in the ceiling.

I had been told earlier by Della Mae that when she died, she wanted me to have her cremated and then buried on her beloved mountains with no fuss or ceremony. And so, after the cremation, I took her ashes and buried them beneath a boulder. I had a special sun dial made that was imbedded into the top of the rock for travelers to see. That rock was split the next summer by a bolt of lightning and the sundial was damaged. I brought the sundial down and had it fixed; I have been planning to reset it."

Susan asked Emily if she would go with her the next day to see the rock; Emily agreed. With Emily driving, they went to Sugar Loaf. It had been many years since Susan had been there. The old narrow dirt road was now a wide, paved road and the old metal arch over the entry to Sugar Loaf was gone. They started climbing and things looked familiar to Emily, even though (except for her dream) she had never been there before.

They climbed until Emily stopped beside a large, dark boulder that had been split in half. There on the top were holes drilled into the rock where something had been bolted. Susan took out a sundial from her backpack and it fit the holes exactly. "This is the very rock, Emily, and as you can see, the sundial belongs here. After it was damaged by lightning, I had it fixed and promised Della Mae that I would put it back, but I never got around to it." Engraved on the sundial was Della Mae's name and the quote: "Come Light Shine On Me."

Emily still tells Susan her dreams and, rest assured, she has Susan's complete attention.

Figure 7.1   Sun dial at burial site before (top) and after (bottom) repair.

About Lightning

Lightning is the flashing of light produced by the discharge of atmospheric electricity. Myths tell many stories about lightning and thunder. Many cultures have elevated lightning to a godly status or regarded it as a manifestation of a god. In ancient Greece, thunder and lightning were manifestations of Zeus; any spot struck by lightning became sacred. In Indochina, people regard the god of lightning as the most powerful of all gods; this god comes to earth with a stone ax and strikes down those who have offended him.

According to European and American folklore, lightning never strikes twice. German folklore holds that a house harboring a quenched brand from the midsummer bonfire will never be struck by lightning. Some myths attribute extraordinary strength to the person who carries a piece of wood splintered off by lightning. In Maryland, a toothpick made from a splinter of a struck tree was believed to cure toothache.

Native American tribes of the Pacific coast say that lightning is the flash of the Thunderbird's eye. In ancient times in Finland, the god Ukko was the god of thunder and his arrows were lightning.

Lightning can be a summer hazard for mountain hikers. Almost daily, thunderstorms bring brief, but often intense, lightning and downpours. If thunderclouds are building, hikers should leave the ridges and summits and stay away from prominent trees. Crouch low if you are caught in a storm. Your car is a safe haven from lightning as long as you do not lean out of the window.

Lightning-caused fires are one of nature's ways of clearing a forest and giving it new life. Fire ignites in the spruce and fir forests an average of every 300 to 400 years. Although most lightning strikes don't start wildfires, the fires that do occur burn readily and intensely. In September 1999, a herd of elk was fatally struck by lightening in the Mount Evans wilderness area. This group of 56 elk may be a gruesome wildlife record.

Personal Story

My father and I went for a walk over our family farm. We stood on a knob about a mile and a half from the house when the lightning and thunder started. We started running to get back to the farmhouse, but after about half a mile, lightning struck nearby and Dad and I found ourselves lying flat on the hillside. We both joked about how we were now safe because "lightning never strikes the same place twice."

Many years later, my son, Eric, his wife, Niki, and I went for a drive up to Mt. Evans (14,264 feet at the summit) late on a summer day. We saw clouds gathering in the distance, several mountain ranges away, but we figured we had enough time to climb the trail up to the boulder field at the top.

Eric was planning a future hike from Mt. Evans to Guanella Pass and wanted to study the terrain. I climbed behind them at a slower pace; before I could join them at the top, the storm was above us. Eric and Niki scrambled down the hill and met me halfway up the trail. When Eric reached out to take my arm, he got an electric shock. My hair was floating and my wool sweater crackled and snapped; I was a lightning rod. We bounded down the trail and reached the safety of the car with enormous relief.

As a mountain hiker, I have often been caught on mountain peaks by fast approaching thunder storms, but since the Mt. Evans experience, I have respected them.

Thunder and lightning had foiled me three times on hikes to Arapahoe Glacier. One October day, I figured the thunderstorm season was over, so I tried again to reach Arapahoe Glacier, a hike of three miles from the trailhead. I climbed, out of breath from the high altitude, and felt confident that this time I would make it.

Clouds formed ominously, but I thought I had time to finish the trip. Yes, I finally made it, and the view from the top was worth it all! Then snow flakes started to float down. They were followed by thunder. Of course, when there is thunder, you can expect lightning.

I took off as fast as I could to get down the mountain. I covered ground quickly, but I paid a price for it. When I got to my Jeep, I was soaked from the storm, which had turned to rain, and one foot was bloody from jamming into the front of my boot as I raced.

All in all, it was a triumphant trip, but my sore foot reminded me about it for quite some time. Although I lost the big toenail, I had gained sights from the mountain top that would stay with me through the winter.

RAINBOWS

The Rainbow
(Iroquois)

Back when the Earth was created on Turtle's back, Sky Woman gave birth to twin sons, Good-Minded and Bad-Minded. With their birth, good and evil came to the world. The two brothers were in continual battle because Good-Minded worked to create things that were beautiful and Bad-Minded was only interested in disfiguring and destroying.

Good-Minded made the rivers and he placed high hills on the sides of the rivers to guard the flow of the water through the valleys. This infuriated Bad-Minded, and he created a sea monster to travel the rivers and destroy them. Because the sea monster was used to the freedom of the wide seas, he was furious with the hills and the way they restricted him. He writhed through the waters and ripped and tore at the sides of the hills and threw great boulders into the rivers.

When Good-Minded saw this, he worried that the rivers would be blocked and engulfed in deep seas and that the mountains and valleys would become dry and arid. Good-Minded rushed to rescue the rivers. The sea monster tried to escape when he saw Good-Minded because he knew and feared his powers. The monster was unable to return through the destroyed rivers and so he fled to the sky.

Meanwhile, the Sun was peacefully making his colorful trail across the heavens. When the Sun learned what the monster had done, the Sun found him and threw him across the sky and pinned him down to the east and the west. The monster's scales flashed beautiful colors in the light. The Sun was satisfied that the sea monster would never return to the Earth to ruin Good-Minded's creations.

Just at that very time, Thunderer was passing on his way through a storm and saw the monster stretched across the sky. Thunderer admired the beautiful colors of the monster as it arched across the sky, so he picked him up and carried the monster to his lodge. "This will be perfect for the bow of my Lightning Hunter," thought Thunderer.

To this day the sea monster is in the heavens, constantly trying to escape from Thunderer when Thunderer is away directing the storms. But, the ever watchful Sun always sees him and bends him across the sky. Sun paints the monster with the brightest colors so that the monster will be discovered by Thunderer. And so, each time Thunderer finds the monster in the sky, he carries the monster back to his lodge.

During summer showers, when you look at the sky and see the resplendent hues that arch the sky, notice how they fade away when the Sun comes forth. That is only Thunderer taking the monster back to his lodge.

About the Story

Myths about the rainbow exist in most cultures. People have always felt the need to explain natural phenomena and the rainbow, because it is so closely related to rain, has a variety of explanations. For instance, an African belief is that the rainbow is a giant snake that comes out to graze after a rainfall. Another African explanation holds that the rainbow is a sign that never again will the god withhold the rain and bring drought. The Fon tribe believes that treasure can be found where the rainbows end. This is similar to Irish stories about the pot of gold at the end of the rainbow.

In Estonia, the rainbow was thought to be the head of an ox lowered to a river to drink. Ponca Indians believe the rainbow is made of flower petals, a theme common to many other Indian tribes. The Shoshone thought the rainbow was a giant serpent who rubs his back on a dome of ice. The Finns saw the rainbow as the sickle or bow of the thunder god, whose arrow was lightning. People of northern Asia thought the rainbow was a camel with three people on its back: the first beat a drum (thunder), the second waved a scarf (lightning), and the third drew reins causing water (rain) to run from the camel's mouth.

Germanic folklore says the rainbow is the bowl that God used at the time of the creation when He tinted the birds. The Japanese believed the rainbow was "the floating bridge of heaven." Buddhists thought the colors of the rainbow were related to the seven planets and the seven regions of the earth. Christians sometimes linked the rainbow's colors to the seven sacraments. The Bible story of Noah and the flood (Genesis 6–9) culminates with the significance of the rainbow:

I do set my bow in the cloud and it shall be a token of a covenant between me and the earth. And it shall come to pass, when I bring a cloud over the earth, that the bow shall be seen in the cloud. And I will remember my covenant, which is between me and you and every living creature of all flesh; and the waters shall no more become a flood to destroy all flesh.

Personal Story

As a child, I always appreciated the sight of a rainbow and fully believed that there was a pot of gold at the end of it; but it wasn't until much later in life that rainbows really spoke to me emotionally.

We had moved to Colorado and my dream as "the girl of the golden West" was to own a place in the mountains. George and I had looked at many places listed for sale, but none was what we wanted. We wanted to find a place with a lake or stream nearby, remote and private, not part of a subdivision.

Then it happened. One summer day, as I was teaching my literature class at the University of Colorado at Denver, the secretary came into the classroom to give me a note from George: "Got a call from the realtor. He found what we are looking for but we need to get right up there!"

I ended the class quickly, went home, and George and I quickly took off for Nederland, a small town in the mountains where our real estate agent's office was located. We rushed into his office, but he took us outside with a whisper, "We can't talk here."

Outside, he led us to an old beat-up car, which he called his rough-road car. He told us he didn't want to talk about the property in the office where others could hear but he was sure this was the place we were looking for.

We drove through the town of Eldora, reached the end of the pavement, and started up the dirt road. It was rough. When we passed the Hessie fork, the road became a steep and narrow shelf road that wound up the mountain over boulders and loose rock. After several miles we saw the 30-foot falls I often visited from a rocky overlook. He said, "It begins here," and he pointed out a national forest sign that signified the beginning of the property (which included the falls). We drove down a lane and parked, then followed a path to an A-frame building built on the side of the hill. The deck of the building overlooked the North Fork of Boulder Creek, and there was an island in the stream created by the arm of the creek, which had split just above the island. Where the two streams joined again—the falls! We couldn't believe the beauty, the sound of the falls, and the perfect five-acre paradise.

The cabin was a one-room building with a wood cook stove, sink, and glory be—a loft above. As a romantic reader of *Heidi*, this was my dream come true. Just like Heidi, I was going to have a loft!

After looking it all over and exploring the boundaries of the property, we told the real estate agent that we wanted to buy it; we didn't quibble about the asking price. Before we returned to Nederland to sign the contract, an afternoon shower created a brilliant rainbow that arched over the valley. We laughed; we had found our pot of gold at the end of the rainbow.

Back at the office, we signed the papers and gave our agent a deposit. As we were filling out the papers, I noted that the land belonged to a professor in Iowa named Schotelius. We were told that we would be able to close on our Eden in a couple of weeks. This all happened during a severe gasoline shortage and the owner felt that he and his wife wouldn't be able to come out to Colorado to their place in the mountains often enough to keep it.

We drove home and as we came out of the mountains, another rainbow arched above the area we lived in.

We waited patiently for two weeks. Then three. When I could no longer stand it, I called the real estate agent to see what was happening. He told me in an uncomfortable voice that another party had looked at the property with another agent and had signed a contract for more money than the asking price. The owner was deliberating the matter.

I was furious. No one had told us it was a bidding war! All we could do was dash back to the real estate office and sign another contract for more money. When we got home, I called information, found Professor Schotelius's telephone number, and called him. We told him what had happened and asked him not to make any decisions until he saw our second contract.

One week later our agent called and told us that the owner was coming to town and would make his decision after he had met us.

We were to meet the owner and his wife in an office in Boulder in the afternoon. As it happened, I had made arrangements for my class to take a field trip to a park for some nature observation and writing experiences. I didn't have time to change from my field clothes—boots and sports clothes—and maybe that turned out to be a good thing. We met with the folks and they were delightful. We had a lot in common with them, felt the same emotional need for the cabin and land; perhaps my clothes helped, too. We signed, sealed, and closed the transaction that very day. The dream property was ours.

When the signing was over, George and I decided to go up to "our property" and celebrate. Although we were careful on the rough road, we still managed to scrape the bottom of the car in several spots. When we explored our land, we discovered some caves on the other side of the island. We were climbing high on the hill when a summer shower drove us to take refuge under some bushes; as we sat there, giddy with our good luck, we were treated to a special celebration prize—a double rainbow extending over the entire valley. We had found the pot of gold at the end of the rainbow.

Chapter 8

American Folklore

"If you wish your children to think deep thoughts, to know the holiest emotions, take them to the woods and hills, and give them the freedom of the meadows. The hills purify those who walk upon them."

Richard Jeffries (Nature essayist, 1848–1887)

TALL TALES

Greenback Cutthroat Trout

One lovely summer day I was enjoying a hike along a section of the Colorado River where some rocks rose from the middle. As I came around a corner in the trail, I saw an extremely agitated squirrel scampering and scooting back and forth along the bank. I watched him for a while, then looked at the river to see what had attracted him.

There on top of a big rock was a peanut. That was it! The squirrel wanted that nut! Suddenly, the squirrel changed his route and scampered away from the river; then he turned around, dug in his feet furiously, and raced to the river. He took a mighty leap and darned if he didn't land on top of the rock! I was so happy with his success, but decided to stay and watch because I wanted to see how he was planning to get off the rock.

He sat out there in the sun and carefully broke the peanut open and took out the nuts. He stuffed them into the sides of his mouth (I could see the bulges in his cheeks); then he explored his rock. It was a good-sized rock, but nothing special.

I could see that he was now trying to figure out how to get back to the bank. He finally attempted a short-field take off, but I could see he wasn't going to make it. I was prepared to watch him get dunked.

Then a big greenback cutthroat trout flashed out of the water and snatched the squirrel in mid-air. As I stood there stunned, I was even more stunned when I saw that greenback cutthroat trout's head come out of the water and carefully place a peanut on the rock.

About the Story

Because the first visitors, explorers, and settlers were amazed by the sights that greeted them in the New World, the United States abounds with tall tales filled with creatures, people, and places larger than life. How could the typical Englishman visiting the geysers in what is now Yellowstone National Park convey to those at home, who knew only gentle, rolling pastures, what he had seen? He *had* to be stretching the truth! Nothing in their experience could prepare his friends for descriptions of miles and miles of bison, obsidian cliffs, steaming vents, spouting geysers, and bubbling mud pots; these were inventions of a fertile mind. And so it was natural for the tall tale to become part of our national culture.

Fishing is part of this larger-than-life tradition. Just *how big* was that fish you caught? Fish stories have become a staple of tall tales—oh, that was just a "fish story."

Recently, the greenback cutthroat trout, which has lived in the streams of the Rocky Mountains for 8,000 years, was named the official state fish of Colorado; it was thought to be extinct until it was found splashing in the South Fork of the Poudre River in 1937. Through the good management of state wildlife officials, the fish has moved from the "endangered" list to the "threatened" category.

Personal Story

Park rangers in the Rocky Mountain National Park tell stories that exhibit the innocence of park visitors. One ranger was floored when a woman from back east asked, "When do the deer turn into elk?" Another visitor asked, seriously, "Who mows the tundra?" Then there was the ranger who was explaining to a group of tourists the story of Moraine Park and Glacier Basin and their geological history. He pointed out the rocks in the valley and said the glacier had deposited them there. One listener asked him, "Where did the glaciers go?" He said he couldn't resist answering the question with "Back to get more rocks." The worst part was that the people in the group accepted this answer. The same ranger also had to answer this statement: "I can't understand how the river got 'way down to the bottom." His replay was, "The river used to be up here on the rim but one day it just slipped off." In Yellowstone National Park, I heard this story from a park ranger as part of the park's bear education talk. It went something like this:

> *Before you start hiking and camping in the back country, there are some safety rules you need to know. They involve avoiding trouble and confrontation with bears. You should wear bear bells on your backpacks so that the bears hear you coming because they will clear out if they get advance warning you are coming. They don't want to meet up with you any more than you want to meet up with them. One of the most dangerous things you can do is to get between a mother bear and her cub; making noises and wearing jangling bells will help you avoid such a happening.*

Should you actually come upon a bear, do not run. I repeat, *do not* run. A bear can catch you in no time. The best thing to do is to drop to the ground and roll yourself up into a ball and cover your head with your hands and arms. If the bear comes up and sniffs you or swats you, don't move; just stay in your tight ball and the bear will lose interest. I know for a fact that this is the wisest advice I can give you.

When I was rather new to the park, another ranger and I were traveling in the back country when we came upon a bear. It was a big one; it stood on its hind legs and towered over us. My friend dropped to the ground and rolled himself up into a tight ball with his arms and hands covering his head. I had a much less controlled response. I ran to a pine tree nearby and started climbing for all I was worth. When I got up a ways in the tree, I stopped to look down and there I saw that bear batting at my friend as he remained motionless in his ball. After about ten swats at him, the bear lost interest and started to pay attention to me; he knew where I was and ambled right up to the tree I was hiding in. With no hesitation, he started to climb that tree; he had no trouble at all because bears have opposable claws. I climbed higher, but the bear was covering the tree trunk trip faster than I was. The next thing I knew, he was so close to me that I could feel his claws scratching my boots, but I shook him off and climbed still higher. The next time his claws grabbed my boots I couldn't shake him off and then I felt him pulling my leg—just as I am pulling yours!

Old Red

Old Red was an amazing hunting dog. He counted birds and would give a bark for each bird. One of the pompous men in town was skeptical about the dog's ability to count. Old Red was such a good bird dog that he would flush the birds out one at a time so that the hunter could take his time shooting them. One townsman doubted this until he saw Old Red in action; he grabbed his gun and crashed through the bush to see how Old Red did it. He found that Old Red had herded the birds into a rabbit hole and had covered the entrance with paw. Old Red then released the birds one at a time.

Later that day, Old Red ran by while shaking a sassafras bush with a knot on the end; he looked like a crazy dog as he hit the townsfolk with the bush. The skeptical fellow, thinking the dog had gone mad, took out his gun and shot Old Red. The owner of Old Red stormed up and roared, "Shoot, he was only trying to tell us that there were more birds than you could shake a stick at out on the lake."

The Split Dog

One of the fellows in town had the best rabbit dog you ever did see. The dog was out running some rabbits one day like he always did, but some lazy lout had left a scythe in the grass with the sharp blade sticking straight up.

The dog was just turning a corner chasing a panicked rabbit when he ran smack-dab into the scythe. The impact split the dog open from the tip of his black nose right straight on down to his tail.

The dog's owner saw him just fall apart so he ran and slapped the dog back together. He jerked off his flannel shirt and wrapped him up in that real quick. He ran to the house and put the dog in a box and poured turpentine all over the shirt.

He kept the dog near the warm stove. When the sun came out, the fellow moved the box with the dog outside. What was amazing was that the dog was breathing a little bit. We all hoped the dog would make it.

After about three weeks, the dog's owner told us that the dog was trying to wriggle now and then, but he kept him wrapped up for another three weeks.

One morning, the owner heard the dog bark; so he started unwrapping him carefully and when he was done, out jumped the dog as spry as ever.

There was only one problem. When the dog's owner had put him together, he had put him upside-down-backwards. He had two legs up and two legs down. But that wasn't a problem at all because the dog turned out to be twice as good a rabbit dog after that. He would run on two legs until he got tired, and then he would just flip himself over and keep right on going. It was an amazing thing to watch that dog run coming and going and barking from both ends!

Old Blue

Old Blue was the best coon and possum hound dog in all the state. All Old Blue's owner had to do was to show the hound a board and Old Blue would go off and find a possum or coon whose hide would fit the board. Old Blue's owner never had to worry about finding a board to fit a hide and he never needed to worry about the quality of the possum or coon skin.

Old Blue disappeared one time for three days. His owner went out to the woods himself to see if he could find any trace of his clever hound. He searched for hours and then just as he was about to quit looking, he found Old Blue. The dog was worn out and exhausted, so Old Blue's owner carried him home cradled in his arms.

Old Blue's owner wondered what had happened to the dog, but he finally figured it out. He saw the problem one day when he went out on the back porch and saw his wife's ironing board leaning against the porch. Old Blue must have seen it and gone out in the woods and wore himself to a frazzle trying to find a possum or coon with a hide big enough to fit that ironing board.

Dead Dog

Down home, there was this fellow who had a wonderful rabbit dog. That dog was the best dog the fellow had ever had, and he had some good dogs before. The dog died. The fellow decided that he had to do something special to remember the dog, so he skinned him and had his wife make a pair of gloves out of the dog's hide. He used those gloves regularly and it always made him think of his rabbit dog.

The fellow was out in the forest working one day and he pulled his gloves off and laid them down on an oak stump. He sat down on another oak tree stump to eat his lunch. Just as he was biting into his sandwich he saw a rabbit run out of the underbrush and before his astonished eyes, the two gloves jumped off of the stump and grabbed the rabbit as it went by and choked it to death.

Personal Story

Wintering the Old Folks

It was perfect. When I made my mind up that our family needed a retreat in the Rocky Mountains, I had high expectations. However, our Taiga Sampo (magic mill) was better than I ever expected. We called it Taiga Sampo after the magic mill in the Finnish epic *The Kalevala.* It surely was a magic mill grinding out dreams and joy. The first summer there we met most of the other residents of the valley. The old gold miners who first settled in the valley called it "Happy Valley." Many of the people living there today are descendants of the original settlers. They consider the valley sacred. We felt the same way.

One of the strongest characters in the valley was a 95-year-old woman called Virginia Gale. Her father had driven the stagecoach that used to connect the mines and settlements in the valley. She knew the history of every place and everyone. She accepted us after my husband saved the life of a hot-blood who drove his four-wheel-drive truck over a cliff. Virginia said, "I like a man of action. You can depend on them. And you know, Norma, you're fine as frog's hair too, because you washed the dumb bunny's blood off to see where the action was."

We didn't have to tell anyone about how George hauled the unconscious driver out of the truck, which was ready to be swept over the next set of falls. I managed to provide enough first aid to hold the vital fluids inside the body as we rushed the young man to the hospital. One of the neighbors in the cabin on top of Klondike Mountain saw it all and spread the word; when we came back from the hospital we found a party taking place on our deck. It was nice to be accepted with no reservations into this special fellowship.

Virginia herself was no pansy. She loved to walk in the mountains and fish, and was really the ruling matriarch of the mountains. She had two artificial knees. When she was 85, her arthritis troubled her to the point that she declared, "I don't understand how the blamed outhouse manages to move further away. At least, it takes me longer to get there." She went to see a surgeon about getting her painful knees replaced. " 'You're too old for such an operation,' he told me," said Virginia, "but I told him, 'Don't worry, young man, I plan to outlast you and I need knees while I do it.' "

Six weeks after her knees had been replaced, Virginia was walking with the help of canes in her mountain meadow. Her recovery was a source of great pride for the surgeon, who boasted about his success. However, it was Virginia who had done it. Her determination had made his workmanship look good.

Virginia had no patience with incompetence. One of the visitors in a summer cabin got his truck stuck in a mud wallow. He had to be towed out of there by several of the valley men, and Virginia was there to supervise it. She snorted about his predicament with, "He is so dumb he couldn't find a stick with two ends." Her final insult was, "He couldn't even lead a silent prayer." She had no time for poor souls who lacked ingenuity.

After we had spent five summers in this setting, we were all talking about the previous winter. All the cabins were closed up in late fall because the 10 miles of dirt road up to our valley was not plowed. Huge snowdrifts covered the road, rocks, frozen stream, and even some cabins. Virginia put poles in several spots of her cabin to support the roof during the winter. Hardy souls got to their places in winter by skis, snowshoes, or skimobiles.

Virginia had declared, "Last winter there was only a barbed wire fence between us and the Arctic and three of the four strands of wire were down." I asked her what she did during the winter. Where did she go? That had always been a mystery to me. I always saw her '55 Chevy parked in a backyard in Eldora during the winter. She called her car Emmer Gen See because she only used it for emergencies.

Eldora was a small settlement of log cabins in a meadow near the 7,000-foot level. Electricity had made it to Eldora, but that was all. The outhouses still served their function and water had to be carried in or hauled from the creek that had formed the valley. When we snowshoed up to the cabin in winter, we had to leave our Jeep in Eldora. The road ended there, but Virginia's car never showed signs of use.

When I mentioned this to Virginia, she said, "I don't have much need for a car in the winter." Again I questioned her as to where she stayed during the winter. I thought maybe one of her three daughters took her in. She said, "We couldn't make it through a winter together in her dinky apartment." Then she gave me the piercing look of an eagle about to catch a snack and quietly stated, "If you really want to know where some of us spend our winter, come up to my cabin on January ninth." I started to sputter something about the road being drifted over, but she snapped, "I didn't misjudge you, did I?"

That December was full of genuine blizzards, and one storm followed another. In the city down on the plains, we spent hours shoveling out of massive accumulations of snow. When the new year came, I laughed with George about the January meeting at Virginia's cabin. We came up with dozens of reasons as to why she had said what she did. The reason we accepted was that she did not want to answer my question as to where she spent the winter.

However, the morning of January ninth was bright, sunny, cold, and full of blue sky. At breakfast, George wasn't even surprised when I said, "Let's snowshoe up to the cabin today." It seemed as if we were reading each other's minds. So I packed some sliced turkey sandwiches, a thermos of coffee, and some fruit to eat at the cabin. I knew I had some dried soup up there and planned to melt snow to make some for our meal.

We parked the Jeep in Eldora (Emmer Gen See was covered with snow), strapped on our snowshoes, fixed our backpacks, and started up the mountain. We peeled off layers of sweaters and jackets as we progressed. It was hard work clomping up the drifted road. We noticed the tracks of some skimobiles ahead of us. It looked as if the same vehicle had gone up and down a few times—at least the tracks looked like the same machine.

Because the tracks passed our place, we decided to check on Virginia's cabin before we dug a trail to our cabin and cleaned the deck off so we could swing the door open. What a shock to see smoke coming from the chimney of Virginia's cabin! There were all sorts of footprints around the cabin, and the skimobile was there, too. We knocked on the door, and when it swung open we were greeted by Virginia herself. "Well, you did remember. I knew you would. In fact, I just won a six-dollar bet that you would make it."

Inside the warm cabin (the roof poles made space awkward) were four people our age and six people around Virginia's age. "Well, you see," she said, "the six of us come up here for the winter after the holidays. The worst part of the winter is yet to come. Right now our arthritis is more than we want to live with for a while, and besides, our Social Security funds really don't cover food and medicine. That's why we choose to take it easy. Watch."

While she was talking, she poured coffee from her blue speckled enamel coffee pot that sat on her wood cook stove for everyone. The six old folks were huddled close to the fire. One of the other four went outside several times, and after one of these trips he (it was Ted, the grandson of one of the original valley settlers) said, "It's time."

With that, the six elders shook hands, hugged each other, and started to take their clothes off. They stripped down to their long johns. I stared at George, and he looked uncomfortable, too. The next thing that happened left me in a panic. The old folks went outside and stretched out on their backs with their arms crossed over their bony chests. No one tried to stop them. I ran, or rather, slid, on the snow over to Virginia and hissed, "Get up Virginia! You are going to freeze. Come on, I'll help you get up."

Her words were as sharp as the winds coming over the pass: "I thought I could trust you to trust me." That stopped me cold. Meanwhile, Ted and the other three hauled some planks out of the storage shed and quickly nailed up a wooden box that was six feet by six feet by six feet. They dragged three bales of hay over to the box and then went inside the cabin. The six old people lay there with their eyes closed. You could see the circulation in their bodies was slowing down. It showed in the extremities first. Their noses, ears, fingers, and toes turned white. George and I went inside the cabin to plead with the others to do something before it was too late. They just said, "Virginia said we could trust you. Was she wrong?"

For some crazy reason we didn't want to let Virginia down, but at the same time how could we stand by and watch these folks commit suicide? Ted told us to sit down and have more coffee, and he stacked some pine logs on the fire. It blazed up with sparks and pops. And there we sat. Why? What was going on? Why were we allowing it happen?

Ted went outside after a while and came back with the announcement that it was time. We went outside knowing full well that those frail old bodies were indeed frozen. Funny, they all had a little smile on their faces. Ted and his brother opened one of the hay bales and spread hay on the bottom of the wooden box. Then they stacked the bodies of the old folks in layers, like cordwood, head to toe. They layered bodies and straw until the box was topped off with straw and then a rough lid. They nailed it down and then went back into the cabin. They put the fire in the stove out and closed things up. Ted made three trips down the mountain on the snowmobile with a passenger each time. His last words as he passed us on his final trip was, "Come back up on May ninth if you want to see the rest."

George and I never did stop at our cabin, let alone eat our lunch. We just plowed down the hill, silently got in the Jeep, and drove back to the city. The rest of that winter was bitter cold, and we both seemed to be suffering with the memories of what we had been part of. How could we have stood by and let it all happen? What kind of people had we become that we could still sleep peacefully at night? And so winter passed into a late spring. Up in the mountains, we knew, it was still winter until near the end of May. There we were once more, with a silent understanding, getting ready to go up to Virginia's on the morning of May ninth. It was raining in the city, but the rain was sloppy-wet snow in the mountains.

When we parked the Jeep in a dug-out area off the road, I remembered we hadn't even packed a lunch. Somehow, food was the last thing we wanted. We knew what we were probably going to see, and it left us solemn. The snow had been packed down by cross-country skiers and a snowmobile. Yes, the tracks looked like the same ones as before.

We didn't hurry our trip. Our cabin looked beautiful when we passed it. The snow reached up to the top of the roof on the upper hillside. We had let the winter pass without coming up once. Yep, at Virginia's there were shoveled spots by the door, smoke curling up on the breezes from the chimney, and outside the big wooden box was covered with snow. Inside the cabin was Ted and his brother and the two other fellows from January. They offered us some coffee and didn't seem surprised at all that we were there.

On the way up to Virginia's, George had mumbled that the ground would still be too frozen to dig any graves. He said that the bodies would never be buried unless someone brought up some dynamite. What haunting images flashed through my mind! It reminded me of the story Virginia had told us about the mine tunnel across the island on our land. She had told us that a determined miner had run it back in 1868 as a one-man operation. He blasted, hauled, and dug enough gold out of it to make a modest profit. When he missed his weekly trip to the town store for supplies, one of his friends became concerned. He went up to the mine to see if the miner was all right. The cabin was empty and the door was open. When he went over to the tunnel he was horrified to see blood and bones splattered all over the rock walls and ceiling. He rode his horse back into town to tell the sheriff that his buddy had blown himself to bits. They figured that the miner had made a careless move with the dynamite. However, the sheriff knew the miner to be a perfectionist and didn't believe he had had an accident. The sheriff went to the mine, carried out all the bits and pieces of the body he could find, took them to the stream, washed them off, and pieced them together. His efforts paid off, because the skull had bullet holes in it. Virginia said that the sheriff never let the case go until he had found the killer and seen him convicted for his crime.

Who would pay for the crimes of letting six old folks die? Ted shoveled the snow off the box and from around it. He then took a crowbar to the top of the box and splintered the lid off. While he was doing that, the other three were spreading clothes out to warm in front of the fireplace. They also had three copper tubs in the cabin. These copper tubs were of the large size that my mother used to boil our clothes in on washdays. People who had lived through the diphtheria epidemic were germ conscious. There were two more tubs outside. They also had big kettles of water boiling over the fireplace.

Ted and his brother lifted the first old stiff body out of the box. It hadn't changed over the winter. They balanced it in one of the outside tubs and started to pour lukewarm water over it. When it bent enough, they scrunched it into the tub and continued to pour water over it. While they did that, they took turns massaging the arms, legs, and body. I couldn't help giving a Virginia-like snort and commenting, "Now is a fine time to worry about what we did." I found myself including George and me in the "we." I was not prepared for what happened next. The old body started to lose its parchment-white color and turned pink. When I heard a cough coming from the body, I almost believed in ghosts. There, before our eyes, the old man opened his eyes and slowly, with a slur in his voice, said, "What a nice sleep. I'm ready to warm up now." They took him inside the cabin, put him in one of the tubs there, and filled that tub up with warm water. This continued until all the old folks had been thawed out. They changed into dry, warm clothes, drank coffee, and inquired as to what the winter had been like. Virginia twinkled at me, "Now you see what we do with old folks in the winter up in Eldora."

About the Story

I developed this story from a tall tale, "Frozen Death," from *Whoppers, Tall Tales and Other Lies* (Schwartz 1975). The tale originated in a Vermont newspaper article in 1887. Details about a real mountain valley, its real inhabitants, and real mining lore were added to the three-page story. Invariably after a telling, people quietly come up to me and ask intently, "Is that a true story?"

I have told this story since 1979, when we bought the cabin above Eldora and met a local legend, whose name I have changed to protect her. Later, life imitated fiction in the mountain town of Nederland, just five miles from Eldora. A young immigrant from Norway had moved to Nederland. When his grandfather, Bredo Morstol, died in 1994, the grandson had him "cryonically" frozen and stored on ice at his Nederland home; the grandson hoped that Bredo could be brought back to life in the future when science had figured out how to do it. Two Boulder filmmakers recently made this true story into the film, *Grandpa's in the Tuff Shed*.

Meanwhile, the grandson has moved back to Norway leaving his grandfather, Bredo, frozen in Nederland. Every third Wednesday for the past three years, Bo Shaffer has hauled 750 pounds of dry ice from south Denver to Bredo's shed. Inside the shed is a large plywood box topped with sheets of foam insulation, two tipped-over sawhorses, a pine bough (Bredo's Christmas tree), and a brandy snifter with a highball glass. Definitely an extended version of "Wintering the Old Folks."

"Wintering the Old Folks" by Norma J. Livo, in *Storytelling Process and Practice* (Littleton, Colo.: Libraries Unlimited, 1986), 160–166.

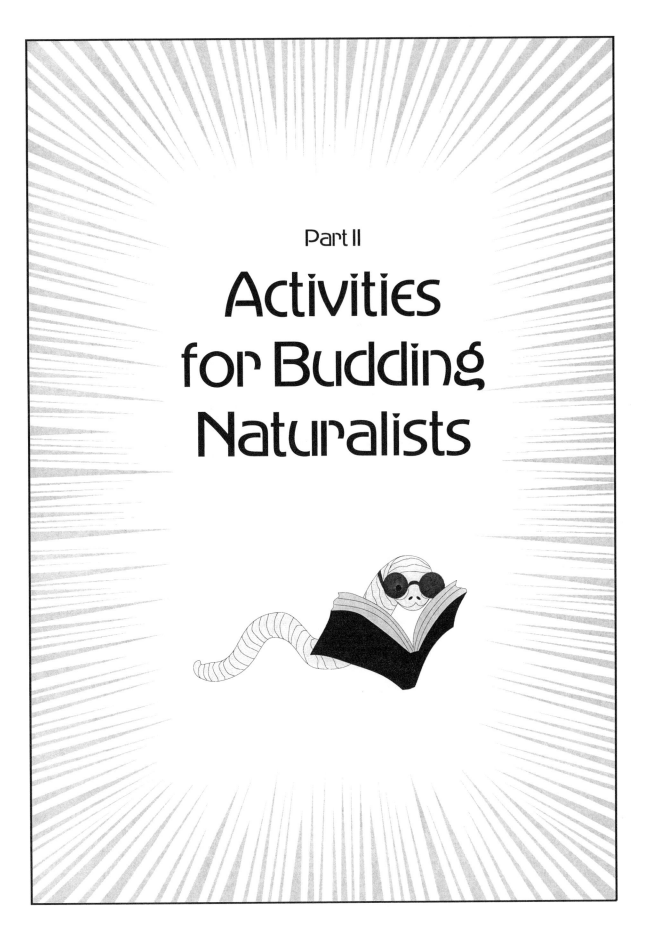

Part II

Activities for Budding Naturalists

Activities to Increase
Naturalistic Intelligence

"Those who want to leave an impression for one year should plant seeds. Those who want to leave an impression for 10 years should plant a tree. But those who want to leave an impression for 100 years should educate a human being."

Chinese proverb

HOWARD GARDNER'S THEORY OF MULTIPLE INTELLIGENCE

Probably the best explanation of Howard Gardner's theories of intelligence is this statement: It's not how smart you are, it's how you are smart. Children who are nature smart care about animals and the environment. They may be more interested in studying plants and leaves or in spending free time recycling.

They have the ability to recognize parts of the natural environment, like clouds or rocks. Some kids are experts on dinosaurs. They have the ability to differentiate the patterns and characteristics among natural objects in the environment and make distinctions in the natural world.

As Socrates said, "We learn when we recognize what we know." To develop this recognition, we must encourage students to observe, record, organize, and analyze information.

Students who exhibit the naturalist tendencies

- see patterns in the world around them;

- nurture, preserve, and protect the natural world;

- are comfortable outside;

- are patient observers of natural phenomena;

- are collectors of such things as rocks, shells, fossils, butterflies, feathers, etc.;

- hypothesize about relationships between natural things;

- like to touch and explore things;

- like to conduct hands-on experiments;

- notice changes in creatures and the environment;

- have a sense of organization for details;

- enjoy drawing and recording information;

- analyze the information they have observed, recorded, and collected;

- have the ability to describe perceptions and observations;

- enjoy subjects, shows, and stories that deal with animals or natural phenomena;

- are aware of their surroundings and changes in it;

- notice similarities, differences and changes in the natural world;

- enjoy camping, hiking, climbing and other outdoor activities;

- have keen sensory skills;

- care about animals and plants;

- learn more about where, when, and how to see wildlife;

- discover wildlife habitats;

- use field guides and other equipment such as binoculars, telescopes, microscopes, magnifiers, and cameras;

- resemble a detective when examining and interpreting wildlife;

- collect data and labels and mount specimens from nature;

- keep logs or journals; and

- observe life without idealization or the avoidance of the ugly.

Through the ages, people who possessed a very strong naturalist intelligence have contributed to our sense of adventure, wonder, and knowledge of the world around us. Such people include the explorers Lewis and Clark, Charles Darwin, John Muir, Rachel Carson, George Washington Carver, Luther Burbank, Annie Dillard, John James Audubon, Aldo Leopold, Enos Mills, and Roger Torrey Peterson.

Gardner believes we can all get better at each of the intelligences, but some people have a better brain for a particular intelligence or their culture gave them a better teacher.

For educators, generating awareness and experiences that enhance the naturalist intelligence are best achieved by combining as many of Gardner's intelligence factors as possible, thereby creating synergy. Recognizing this naturalist intelligence allows us to plan educational programs that will enable children to reach personal goals; it also helps teachers reach more children who are eager to learn and profit from learning material in several ways. The integration of reading, writing, listening, speaking, mathematics, literature, science, and social studies will enrich the naturalist's learning.

Resources are available for helping the budding naturalist: they include the National Audubon Society, Boy Scouts of America, Girl Scouts of the USA, the Izaak Walton League of America, U.S. Department of Agriculture Forest Service, The National Park Service, natural history museums, observatories, parks, planetariums, and zoos.

STORYTELLING

Storytelling has power. When you tell a story, the audience becomes a part of the telling. Storytelling is an ancient concept containing patterns, shapes, subpatterns, and subshapes of the overall story. All stories conform to the rules that govern story structure or they would not be stories. Storytelling transforms and transmits information to the listener; it transcends time and orders events to make existence more sensible and meaningful; it brings a higher level of comprehensibility to the things we are learning.

Storytelling is a unique and natural human activity, an art form, and an immediate experience. One of the most important aspects of storytelling is the sharing of imagination; not only that of the storyteller but also of the listener.

Storytelling is the oral presentation of experiences, myths, fables, folktales, folklore, biographies, parables, aphorisms, and fiction. Teachers are often surprised to learn how carefully students listen to stories. Throughout the world, parents use storytelling to teach their children survival skills and to help meet their emotional needs. Storytelling and stories teach listeners that everything they do has a consequence.

Many groups and books share and teach the art of storytelling: it is an activity open to anyone of any age to develop, share, and enjoy. We have as much need for storytelling today as we always have because oral sharing is our inheritance and our invention.

In the age of television and computers, we easily forget that storytelling gives meaning to our lives and experiences. Storytelling

- provides a much-needed opportunity for adults and students of all ages to interact on a very personal level;

- develops in the student storyteller an awareness of and sensitivity to the information, thoughts, and feelings of listeners;

- stimulates imagination and visualization;

- helps develop poise in the student storyteller; and

- improves discrimination in the choice of materials and stories and fosters increased knowledge.

To learn storytelling techniques:

- Invite a storyteller to your class; ask him or her tell some stories and explain the process of developing a story. Do not forget to include old-timers with good stories among your guests.

- Have the students pay special attention to how your storyteller deals with characterization, mood, atmosphere, setting, and style.

- Have your students practice telling stories to youngsters of different ages.

How can you evaluate storytelling? Encourage students to participate in ongoing objective evaluations of storytelling. If possible, videotape a storyteller telling a story and ask the students to evaluate the teller and discuss their findings. Have the students develop a checklist for their evaluations. A sample checklist might read as follows:

- Motivate the audience to listen

- Convey action vividly

- Convey sequence of events clearly

- Assume a character's point of view
- Express motives
- Express conflict
- Express human values
- Establish mood
- Use figurative language
- Use language rhythmically
- Speak clearly and distinctly
- Use varied intonation
- Use appropriate gestures
- Use eye contact effectively
- End the story gracefully

But probably the most important part of successful storytelling is to tell a story you really enjoy. Use storytelling as an important tool to reach students and to teach them.

Observation and Recording

Field observation and recording of information, a research tool used by scientists and writers, nurture the naturalist learner. What do creatures look like? Do they appear to be in good physical health? How does the animal, bird, or insect move? What sounds does a creature make? How can you describe them? Is there an interaction between the resident creatures? What is that interaction? Are the creatures frightened off by an observer? What are the critters' activities? Is the activity brief or sustained?

There are many ways to record information. No matter which method you choose, recording information should be a pleasure, not a chore. Recording techniques include keeping a journal, filling in a log, taking photographs, drawing, taping, developing charts and checklists, and keeping a scratch pad. Deadlines are artificial in observing and recording. Let memories and other experiences jog the information you record; a good observer knows that no detail is unimportant.

There are no fixed rules to record-taking. Students can develop their own methods of recording information tailored to the job at hand; this will help them organize their thoughts and their expectations. What details do they expect to observe?

Various situations may cause the observer to expect certain patterns. How can the student properly summarize and generalize data? Should the results become a report, a story, or a list of facts?

The combination of storytelling, observation, and recording creates a strong foundation on which to build other experiences.

Storytelling Journal

Storytelling and recording can be a combined activity. Start a storytelling journal to document your storytelling activities; include programs, announcements, and other material about events held at schools, libraries, museums, or community organizations.

In your journal you could record the sources of the stories you heard at an event. Which stories dealt with animals, plants, natural events, or stars and planets? Make copies of stories you heard and document their relationships to nature.

Keep notes about storytelling sessions; record new story ideas and any storytelling ideas you learned. It might help in the future if you have a record of that great line you thought of when you were in the middle of telling a story. Sometimes we get flashes of insight and invent wondrous variations while in action. Sometimes the story reveals itself to us while we are listening to it or telling it.

This journal should serve as a progress report of your storytelling. It can remind you of things that worked or did not work, and document your development as a storyteller. You can record family stories that you might be able to develop; you can jot down ideas for original stories. You will probably refer to this journal often as you develop your repertoire of stories.

Format

Loose leaf photograph albums with plastic overlays make convenient journals. The album is flexible and allows you to insert and rearrange pages; the pages also protect newspaper articles, which tend to deteriorate. Whatever format you choose for your journal, the important thing is to start your journal *now*.

IDEAS FOR ACTIVITIES

In the following sections, you will find activities related to the stories told earlier as well as ways to integrate them into curricula. Encouraging and nurturing naturalists abounds with rich possibilities.

To start with, display questions for young naturalists to research, observe, and explore:

- Why do animals live where they live?

- How many kinds of animals live in the world?

- How can animals live in the desert?

- Why do camels have humps?

- Why don't birds' feet freeze in winter?

- Why do elephants have big ears?

- What is ecology?

- Why do cockroaches usually come out at night?

- Why do some birds have both summer and winter homes?
- What tells animals when to migrate?
- How do migrating animals know where to go?
- Why don't all birds fly south in autumn?
- Why do bats fly at night?
- How can bats see in the dark?
- How do mother animals recognize their own babies?
- How do baby birds recognize their own parents?
- How does a mother bird know in which order to feed her hatchlings?
- What is a tadpole?
- How does a turtle get into its shell?
- Is a pony a baby horse?
- Why do birds sing?
- Why do whales sing?
- Why do wolves howl?
- Why does a woodpecker peck?
- Why do some animals have horns?
- Why does a rattlesnake rattle?
- Why does a cat fluff up its fur?
- Why do animals fight?
- Why do some animals kill others?
- Do animals ever cooperate?
- Do animals talk with one another?
- Can animals think?
- How do birds learn to build nests?
- How do beavers know about dam building?
- How do animals learn to use tools?
- How do insects know that winter is coming?
- What are feelers for?
- Why do cats have sharp claws?
- Why do cats' eyes shine at night?
- How can a hawk see better than we can?
- How do chickens know when it is time to go to bed?

- How can a dog follow a trail with its nose?
- Can animals count?
- What makes electricity in an electric eel?
- How can animals grow new tails?
- How can flies walk on the ceiling?
- How do animals hide from enemies?
- Why do spiders spin webs?
- Do animals have feelings?
- Do animals sleep?
- Do dogs dream?
- Why do bears hibernate?
- What makes a weed a weed?

These questions are intended to prime the pump of the student's thinking and exploring.

Interviewing people for the creatures they like the most and the creatures they like the least could be one of your initial activities. What reasons did people give for their choices? Develop a chart to document the most frequent choices.

Chapter 1: Amphibians and Reptiles

Snakes

Have your students study the following list:

- Two examples of the way snakes stir the imagination can be seen at Serpent Mound, Ohio, and Snake Path on the University of California-San Diego campus. Serpent Mound, an ancient quarter-mile-long (0.4 km) mound representing a serpent, is located near Hillsboro, Ohio. Adena Indians built Serpent Mound sometime between 800 B.C.and A.D. 1, but the significance of the mound is unknown. Artist Alexis Smith built a modern "Snake Path" on the University of California-San Diego campus. Hexagonal slate tiles, arranged like scales, cover the 560-foot-long (170m) path. This serpent even has a pink granite tongue. One of these snake representations is very old; the other, very modern. What reasons can you think of that inspired the Adena Indians to make the giant Serpent Mound? What may have inspired modern artist Alexis Smith to create the Snake Path? How do you think the reasons for these two creations are similar? How are they different?

- With the help of a field guide to reptiles, learn which snakes live in your state or province. How many species are harmless? How many species are venomous? How can you tell the harmless species from the venomous species?

- Astronomers divide the night sky into constellations. The constellation Serpens (the serpent) depicts a large snake. An assorted constellation, Ophiuchus, represents a man who holds the snake's head with his left hand and the tail with his right hand. Serpens contains the stars Alpha Serpentis and Theta Serpentis and the star cluster M16. Using a field guide to the night sky, locate Serpens and Ophiuchus. Observers in the Northern Hemisphere have a good view of these constellations in July.

- Many regional societies specialize in snakes and other reptiles and amphibians. Contact the Society for the Study of Amphibians and Reptiles (SSAR) for information about societies in your area: SSAR Regional Societies, Eric M. Rundquist, Sedgwick County Zoo, 5555 Zoo Boulevard, Wichita, KS 67212.

- We tend to think of snakes as dangerous, even as killers; and a very small minority are. An article in *Men's Health* magazine in February of 1992 gives the statistics of deaths in the United States through encounters with animals for 1991. These are numbers of human deaths caused by various wild animals: deer, 131; bees, 43; dogs, 14; rattlesnakes, 10; spiders, 4. Deaths were also caused by sharks, captive elephants, scorpions, rats, goats, captive leopards, jellyfish, coral snakes, alligators, grizzly bears, mountain lions, captive monkeys, stingrays, vultures, and killer whales. Deer, of course, we do not think of as being dangerous. They do, however, tend to run into or in front of cars and cause fatal accidents. Make a graph of these findings. Instead of using words to represent the animals, make drawings or collect pictures.

- Poisonous snakes in the United States do not pose a great problem so far as human mortality is concerned, but other countries are not as lucky. It is estimated, for example, that the cobra kills about 10,000 people in India each year. Pretend that you are planning to visit India. Research the precautions you should take to prevent yourself becoming a statistic.

- Many snakes are beautifully decorated. Look in a good field guide that has photographs or drawings of snakes in color. Copy a pattern that you like and use it in designing a book cover.

- Snakes are probably the first things we made when we started to work with clay. The basic technique of rolling clay under one's hand to form a cylindrical shape is easily learned. Go a step further. Fashion a clay snake that looks as realistic as you can make it. Students interested in origami can try folding a paper snake.

- Snakes vary greatly in length, from about six inches (15 centimeters) to 33 feet (10 millimeters). Make a chart that documents the lengths of snakes. Research the speed of various snakes and make a chart showing this information.

- Almost without exception, snakes are, by human standards, poor parents. Young snakes fend for themselves from birth. Pretend that you are a crusader determined to make better parents of snakes. Write a parents' manual for snakes. Illustrate it with drawings.

- Write an essay titled "How to Appreciate Snakes."

- Choral readings about snakes can be fun. For effect, exaggerate every sibilant "s" in the reading so that the hiss of the snake is a dominant feature. Create your own choral reading and perform in front of an audience.

Chapter 2: Birds

The next list will inspire your students to sharpen their skills in observing birds:

- Build a bluebird house. Patterns are available for building them; check at lumber or hardware stores for such plans.

- Read "Bird Couple's Vow" and then read "Jack and the King's Girl" from the classic collection *The Jack Tales* by Richard Chase (Houghton Mifflin, 1943). How are these stories alike? How are they different? Develop a chart and list under a column heading "Alike" what makes the stories alike. Under a column heading "Difference," list the ways the stories are different. Write an original story in which someone cleverly outsmarts someone else.

- Primitive cultures considered birds magical creatures. Unlike humans and other beasts, birds were not earthbound but could soar through the heavens. Many cultures even worshipped birds and believed that they could bring rain, predict the future, and bring good or ill luck. Create your own magical bird by developing a composite bird with a variety of heads, bodies, tails, legs, feet, etc.

- The song of the bird is the song of hope. Nature and bird songs combine in many musical masterpieces. The following music selections are excellent examples of where bird songs are perfectly mixed and matched to lilting classics. You may not be able to tell where nature's tune stops and human masterpieces begin.

  "Bird Songs at Eventide" (Coates)

  "Tropical" (Gould)

"The Maiden and the Nightingale" (Granados)

"Ballet of the Chicks in Their Shells" from *Pictures at an Exhibition* (Mussorgsky, with arrangement by Ravel)

Suite: *The Birds; Prelude, the Dove, the Hen, the Nightingale, and the Cuckoo* (Respighi)

Listen to some of these classical pieces and analyze the music for the bird songs. How would you describe it? How can you tell someone how the music makes you feel?

- Recently, as part of the Colorado Symphony's *Amazing Arts Discovery* series, the symphony and the Denver Zoo created a musical field trip. The orchestra performed vignettes, each featuring a different animal. Each animal, from the great horned owls to boa constrictors, were presented on stage by zoo representatives. Video cameras televised close-up pictures of the animals on three big screens so that everyone in the audience got a good view. These vignettes were enchanting and wonderfully creative. After the concert, the symphony director and a zoo representative presented a question-and-answer session; its purpose was to show how valuable and deserving of our respect the bird and animal world is. Ask your music teacher whether you could present such a program at your school (with your school band or orchestra providing the music). Brainstorm the different ways you could accomplish such a project.

- Obtain a bird field guide and take a bird-watching field trip. Make a list of the birds you observe.

- During your trip, watch for sound and movement. When you spot a bird, keep your eyes on it. Note its basic shape and posture. Does it have a long tail or a thick beak? Is its beak long? What color is it? Does it have a pattern or stripes? What color is the bird? How is its face marked? Does the bird hold its tail up, down, or flip it around? Some birds are easy to recognize; others will need a field guide to help you identify them.

- Locate a book on birds of each of the states. How many states have the same bird as its state bird?

- There are opponents and proponents to feeding birds. Contact your state wildlife department and find out how they feel about feeding birds. What are some concerns?

- Why put feeders up in the fall and take them down again in the spring?

- If you do decide to put up a bird feeder, situate it in an open area with trees or shrubs nearby to provide shelter and cover. Which predators must birds cope with?

- Squirrels provide a problem for bird feeders; devise or invent a technique to keep squirrels away from feeders.

- Birds can transmit diseases to each other at feeders. What are some of the things you can do to prevent spreading diseases through the use of a feeder?

- What kind of foods are best for use in feeders? Find recipes for bird feed, such as a soft peanut butter mix, or suet tidbit cakes.

- Collect pictures of different birds. Use them to develop a poster to match birds with their descriptions.

- If you want to learn more about the language of humans, listen to songbirds. Research has shown that much of the complex vocalizations of some songbirds is learned behavior and possibly provides a model for understanding how humans learn to speak. For example, like humans, the white-crowned sparrows of the western United States have been found to develop a "dialect," depending on where they live. A trained listener can distinguish among sparrows from Marin County, Berkeley, and Sunset Beach, California. On a bird field trip, take along an audio tape recorder. Collect a tape of sounds of the birds. Play it back to others to see if they can identify the birds on the tape.

- Resident ducks and domestic geese, mallards, widgeons, and wood ducks benefit parks, especially during spring, summer, and fall. Their main food sources are weeds and weed seeds. They also eat insects, including mosquitoes and their larvae. What are some foods that are dangerous for the birds to eat?

- Study a map of your state and make a list of place names that refer to birds. Research how these places got their names.

- Create origami waterfowl to hang in the classroom, library, or your own bedroom (see Figure 9.1).

Waterfowl

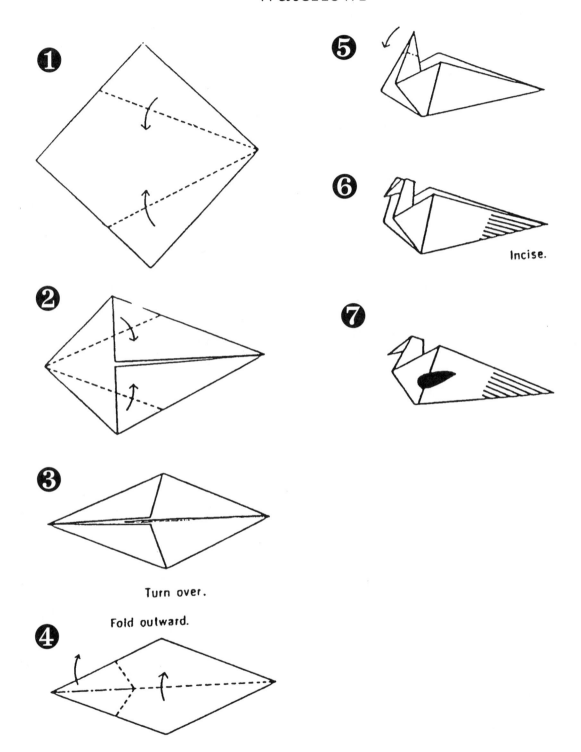

Figure 9.1   How to fold an origami waterfowl.

- Read the following piece (author unknown) titled *Lessons on Teamwork from Geese*:

> Fact 1. As each goose flaps its wings it creates an "uplift" for the birds that follow. By flying in a V-formation, the flock gains 71 percent greater flying range than if each bird flew alone.
>
>> Lesson. People who share a common direction and sense of community can get where they are going faster and more easily because they are traveling on the thrust of one another.
>
> Fact 2. When a goose falls out of formation, it feels the drag and resistance of flying alone. It quickly moves back into formation to take advantage of the lifting power of the bird immediately in front of it.
>
>> Lesson. If we have as much sense as geese, we will stay in formation with those headed where we want to go. We are willing to accept their help and give our help to others.
>
> Fact 3. When the lead goose tires, it rotates back into the formation and another goose flies to the point position.
>
>> Lesson. It pays to take turns doing the hard tasks and sharing leadership. As with geese, people are interdependent on each other's skills, capabilities, and unique arrangements of gifts, talents and resources.
>
> Fact 4. The geese flying in formation honk to encourage those in front to keep up their speed.
>
>> Lesson. We need to make sure our honking is encouraging; in groups where there is encouragement, the production is much greater. The power of encouragement (to stand by one's heart of core values and encourage the heart and core of others) is the quality of honking we seek.
>
> Fact 5. When a goose is sick, wounded, or shot down, two geese drop out of formation and follow it down to help and protect it. They stay with it until it dies or is able to fly again. Then they launch out with another formation or catch up with the flock.
>
>> Lesson. If we have as much sense as geese, we will stand by each other in difficult as well as good times.
>
> "Can we honestly say that we are as smart as geese?"

Discuss the truth of the facts. If possible, watch a formation of geese flying. Are the lessons something of importance? Can you develop a list of facts and lessons based on another animal?

Chapter 3: Four-Footed Animals

"If we cease to wander the hills and feel the earth beneath our feet, we face the possibility of understanding less and less about ourselves and the planet where we walk."

Roger "Sandy" Sanborn, Cofounder of Sanborn Western Camps (near Florissant Fossil Beds National Monuments, Florissant, Colo.)

Coyote Activities

- Read Chapter 5 in *Roughing It* by Mark Twain. This contains a simultaneously contemptuous and humorous account of coyotes. How have attitudes about coyotes changed since Twain's time? How have they stayed the same?

- Sometimes national parks are good places to see coyotes. Because coyotes are protected in the parks, they often have little fear of people and can be observed closely. Park Service policy prohibits harassment of wildlife, so if you encounter coyotes (or any other wildlife), keep your distance while you observe.

- The words we use affect our feelings about things. Write a paragraph about coyotes using the words from the left column below. Rewrite the paragraph, but this time use the words from the right column.

"Good" or Neutral Words	"Bad" Words
inhabit	infest
hungry	bloodthirsty
shy	sly
single-minded	ruthless
hunt	stalk
prey	victim
wild animal	varmint
creep	slink
adaptable	indiscriminate

Wolf Activities

Wolves have suffered from stereotyping. Study the following list to familiarize yourself with ways wolves have been stereotyped:

- Brainstorm all the things you think or feel when the word *wolf* is mentioned. If your reaction is mostly negative, reflect and discuss why this might be.

- Bring in pictures of wolves. Are there stereotypes? How is the stereotyping of wolves similar to that of human beings or of different countries and cultures?

- Which other animals suffer from stereotyping? (For example, pigs and turkeys.) Why are they stereotyped? Write a story stereotyping another animal.

- Brainstorm positive aspects of wolves. Research the literature for additional positive aspects of wolves.

- Create posters or bumper stickers with slogans that encourage positive feelings toward wolves.

- Brainstorm remedies to the stereotyping of wolves. Get together in small groups and discuss what you can do to eliminate the stereotyping.

Wolves and the Environment

- Discuss how animals adapt to new environments and the possible consequences of their not adapting.

- Research wolf tracks. Make a transparency of the tracks. Discuss how wolves hide or escape from their predators.

- Discuss preparations wolves make for winter. Illustrate their preparations on a poster.

- Keep an imaginary journal for five days about the life of a wolf.

- Make a concentration game with cards, half showing pictures of animals, the other half their habitats.

Wolves as an Endangered Species

- Brainstorm the things you think have contributed to wolves becoming endangered.

- Research the laws in your state concerning the killing of wolves. How have these laws changed?

- Research the reason wolfhounds were bred.

- Collect newspaper and magazine articles about the studies or research done on wolves or their reintroduction into former habitats. Use this information for a bulletin board on wolves.

- Relate the similarities and differences of what is happening to the wolf today and what has happened in the past. Refer to current newspaper and magazine articles and books like *The Last Wolf of Ireland* by Elona Malterre (New York: Clarion, 1990).

- Discuss the impact of restrictions on killing wolves. Predict what you think the future holds for wolves.

- Write an article or advertisement describing the wolf and convince your audience of the importance of its existence.

- Make a poster that charts what you have learned in your research.

Wolves and the Arts

- Sculpt a wolf from clay. Make a mural of wolves in the wild as a backdrop for the sculpture.

- Make wolf puppets. Produce a puppet play advertising the wolf to convince the audience of the importance of the wolf's survival. Write a song about wolves to include in the play. Build a wolf mask and use it in a play or song presentation.

Wolves in Literature

- Investigate the legend of the werewolf. Where did it come from? Do people still believe it?

- Assemble a stack of children's books and comics about or including wolves. Look through and divide them into "wolves that are real" and "wolves that are unreal." Share examples of both. Name three things an imaginary animal does that a real animal cannot do. Discuss what makes animals real and what makes them unreal.

  1. Discuss the importance of being able to tell when something is real and when something is make-believe. Discuss why this distinction is important to remember when learning about animals and how they live.

  2. Compare examples of animals as portrayed in these books and comics for a variety of categories: sounds they make, shelter, appearance, actions, food, movement, etc. Chart these examples.

- Several picture books of *Peter and the Wolf* are available. Compare and contrast these different books with the musical piece by Sergei Prokofiev. How are they alike? How are they different? Play the music and discuss which instrument represents what character in the story. Describe what the instruments sound like. Discuss other ways to portray animals with other musical instruments. Act out the story.

- Read several folk stories with wolves as the main characters. Discuss where the stories take place, exploring the geography and environment.

- Libraries have a variety of books based on the story of *Little Red Riding Hood.* (Ask a librarian to help you collect some of these books.) Compare and contrast these different versions. Repeat this task for the story of *The Three Little Pigs,* including Jon Scieszka's *The True Story of the Three Little Pigs,* which is told from the wolf's point of view. Rewrite a folktale from the point of view of the wolf. Variations of this activity could include newspaper articles, society page articles, letters to Ann Wolfers, a mock trial for a wolf, and so forth. You could rewrite a folktale while concentrating on using synonyms, for example, "Little Red Riding Hood initiated plans for the preparation, transportation, and delivery of nutritious gifts to a senior citizen relative."

- Adapt a folktale with a wolf as one of the main characters into a Readers' Theatre script. Use the following script as an example, but create your own script.

Readers' Theatre: The Dog and the Wolf

Cast of Characters:
Narrator
House Dog (a pet)
Wolf

Narrator: Aesop, a slave in the sixth century B.C., collected and told many fables. It was said that he won his freedom by his storytelling talents. "The Dog and the Wolf" is adapted from Aesop's fable of the same name. The fable begins when a wolf, half-dead with hunger, comes upon a house dog.

House Dog: (energetically) Hey, brother wolf, what's happening?

Wolf: (in a very sad voice) Nothing, lately. In fact, I haven't had anything to eat for days.

House Dog: I can see that! Look at you, you can hardly stand up. You must be weak from hunger.

Wolf: (very weakly) I know, but what can I do? I can never know when or where I'll get my next meal.

House Dog: Now that's a problem. (Pause) Maybe I have a deal for you. Come with me to my master and share my work. The work is hard, but the food is regular and good.

Narrator: And so they went, the jovial, well-fed house dog gaily leading the frail, weak wolf. (Pause) As they were making their way towards the town, the wolf noticed something peculiar about the house dog. He questioned him.

Wolf: Hey, dog, how did the hair on your neck get worn away?

House Dog: Oh, this? (Pointing to one side of his neck) That's nothing. That's where my master puts the collar on me at night when he chains me up. Yes, it rubs a bit, but I do get fed each day. You don't get something for nothing.

Narrator: When he heard this, the wolf suddenly stopped, turned around, and started slowly walking back to where they came from.

House Dog: (impatiently) Hey! Where are you going? You can't leave now. We are going to work together.

Wolf: No way! Good-bye, House Dog. To me it's better to starve free than to be a fat slave.

Narrator: With that, the wolf went on his way to enjoy his free—if sometimes hungry—life.

Elk Activities

The following list suggests activities to help students familiarize themselves with the elk:

- What is the Native American name for elk? ("Wapiti," a Shawnee name that means "white rump.")

- Most cultures tell stories about elk. Check the "398" section of your library for folktales from all over the world.

- Native Americans have hunted elk for thousands of years. Present a report on how they used the bones and the antlers, the hides and the teeth.

- Examine an atlas to find where cities, towns, and counties have been named after the elk.

- Check also for geographic features such as rivers, lakes, buttes, points, and mountains that have been named after elk.

- Research antlers and make a poster of the information you have discovered.

- Investigate the different sounds elk make and discover what they are communicating to each other.

- If you live in an area where you can observe elk, here are some tips:
    1. Leave pets at home.
    2. Always observe elk from a distance. Use binoculars and spotting scopes.
    3. Talk in whispers and minimize sharp sounds such as clicking cameras.
    4. Never come between a cow and her calf.
    5. Stay clear of bulls during their rutting or mating season.
    6. Behave like a guest in their wild home—try not to bother them.

- Interview a biologist to discover what the signs of elk are. How can you tell elk have been in the area?

- Present visual materials about elk such as films, books, or elk objects. Imagine that you are an elk looking for a place to live. Describe what you would like to have available in your habitat.

- Write and illustrate advertisements that offer elk habitat for rent or an elk looking for new habitat. Display the ads.

- Collect news items about elk and place them in a file. Later these articles can be used for a bulletin board or class display.

- Write a newspaper article from the point of view of a carpenter or contractor, motel owner, camping outfitter, hunter, homeowner, the mayor, rancher or farmer, off-road vehicle rider, hiker, dog owner, commuter, highway commissioner, U.S. Fish and Wildlife Service officer, state wildlife manager, elk biologist, tribal leader, radio broadcaster, newspaper reporter, and television reporter. How would the information in the different newspaper articles be alike or different? Why?

- Create a dictionary about elk terminology.

Chapter 4: Constellations

Here are some suggestions for your students to spark their interest in becoming acquainted with the heavens:

- Listen to melodies with haunting outer-worldly sounds. Examples of music of the sun, moon, and stars include

    Theme from *2001: A Space Odyssey* (also "Sprach Zarathustra") (Richard Strauss)

    "Sunrise" from *Grand Canyon Suite* (Ferdy Grofe)

    "Clair de Lune" (Debussy)

    "Venus" from *The Planets* (Holst)

    "Moonlight on the Terrace" (Debussy)

    "Jupiter" from *The Planets* (Holst)

Can you find other pieces of music that refer to planets, stars, the heavens, the moon, and the sun?

- How many constellations can you identify? Where can you find star maps?

- Use a piece of black construction paper and punch holes with a pointed object (needle, pins etc.) to form the Orion constellation. Do the same for other constellations. Place these in a window so that the light shines through the holes. Another way to use these constellations is to darken the room and shine a flashlight from behind the construction paper.

- Get acquainted with the night, as the poet Robert Frost instructed. Observe the brightest stars. What are they? Study the star patterns in the sky from the Big and Little Dipper and the North (Polaris) Star. Draw sketches and report in your journal what you have found.

- The Lakota Indians believed that constellations in the sky signified land forms in the Black Hills, such a Devil's Tower in what is now northeastern Wyoming. As the sun traveled from one constellation to the next, the

Lakota mirrored the sun's movement on Earth by migrating to the corresponding landmarks. Ultimately, the Lakota believed, stellar mirroring allowed them to become one with the universe. Can you discover any of their beliefs in stories about the stars from other tribes and cultures?

• On the first day of spring, the sun moved into a constellation we know as Pleiades, but the Lakota name for it means "Seven Little Girls." The seven-star constellation represented Harney Peak in southwest South Dakota. Because Harney Peak has seven peaks associated with it, each year the Lakota migrated to Harney Peak and performed special ceremonies there when the sun entered Pleiades. The spring journey ended at Devil's Tower, where the entire Lakota nation gathered during the summer solstice to perform the Sun Dance, a sacred, spiritual ceremony. According to Lakota tradition, when the sun actually gets into the Black Hills, ceremonies are being held in the stars by the star people. Can you identify the Pleiades? What do you know about the solstice? Find the Black Hills on a map.

• Oral tradition is important to the Lakota. One legend from their oral tradition tells about Fallen Star. Many, many moons ago, a young Lakota woman who was living in the stars fell through a hole down to Earth. She was pregnant, and when she fell, she died. But her baby was born and was named Fallen Star. He was raised by a bird, a meadowlark. Because the meadowlark was known to speak Lakota, Fallen Star grew up speaking Lakota. Fallen Star was the bringer of high levels of consciousness and knowledge; he traveled from one Lakota band to another, teaching and helping the Lakota people in various ways. Can you find other Native American stories about someone falling from the sky onto Earth? Find some of these stories and compare and contrast them. Do these stories have anything to do with shooting stars?

• Have you ever seen the Milky Way? The Native Americans believe that after they die they go to the heavens and become part of the Milky Way. Find other stories and beliefs about the Milky Way.

Chapter 5: Plants

The following suggestions will guide and inspire your students to learn about plants:

• Find a book on state flowers. Make a list of states that have the same flowers.

• Study the plants that are native to your area.

• Take a nature walk and find as many flowers as you can.

• Sketch and record the different flowers you find.

- Draw pictures and write descriptions of the flower in a flower notebook.

- Look through various resources to identify the names of the flowers you have found.

- Share your results. Did others discover the same flowers? Were there any different discoveries?

- Estimate the number of flowers of a specific species and create a bar graph or pie chart that shows the ratio of one type of flower to the rest of the plant population you found.

- Adopt a tree in a nearby area. Visit the tree regularly. Predict and record what changes they will see during the seasons.

- As the seasons change, compare your observations with your predictions.

- Activities to involve all your senses include collecting, pressing and laminating leaves, making stencils of leaves, and creating bark rubbings.

- Measure as far up the tree as you can reach, as well as the trees' girth. Estimate the size of the rest of the tree (including the root system).

- Why did the Native Americans call aspen trees "the tree that whispers to itself?"

- Why do aspen leaves quake?

- Listen to the sounds you hear in different areas. Does the wind in trees make a special sound? Describe it. Write a poem about it.

- Describe the smells of the forest. Does it smell differently at different times of the year? Are there some trees that have a special smell?

- There are some pieces of classical music that invite you to enter a deep forest, sheltered by fragrant pines, cooled by a sweet breeze, whispering and rustling with life. Listen to some of these pieces, including

  The Four Seasons (Vivaldi)

  Tales from the Vienna Woods (J. Strauss, Jr.)

  Prelude to the Afternoon of a Faun (Debussy)

  "Forest Murmurs" from *Siegfried* (Wagner)

  "Hunt in the Black Forest" (Volke)

- Plant a tree. Water and nurture it and keep a journal documenting your tree's growth and the changes in it.

Chapter 6: Creatures from Water

> "To the Sami (people of Lapland) everything in nature is alive and sacred. Our life and our power flow through us from beyond the sun and stars, from beneath the rocks and waters, and from everything in between. We need each other to survive and grow."
>
> Kristen Madden (Sami)

Fish

The next list will help your students better understand creatures of the water:

- Develop bumper sticker sayings about creatures that live in the water. Some examples:

    Favorite tune of the trout is "Somewhere Over the Rainbow."

    The salmon refuses to go with the flow.

    Catfish hobbies include lounging and goldfish-chasing.

    Swordfish are armed and delicious.

    The lobster is a real hardbody.

    The king crab is the annual winner of the oceanic "great legs" contest.

- There are many sayings about fish; here are some:

    Slippery as an eel.

    Crazy is the fisherman who salts his catch already in the lake (Finland).

    A man will marry a bad wife rather than none at all, as a starving pike will eat a frog (Finland).

    If fish are jumping high, a drizzle is coming (Finland).

    House guests are like dead fish—they begin to stink after three days.

What other saying about fish can you find? Make a list of them.

- Write some riddles that involve fish.

- Listen to some music that might be called "symphonies of the sea." A wealth of music that evokes the motion of waves, the cry of birds, and the almost mystical healing properties the sea possesses. Some musical pieces include:

"Four Sea Interludes" from *Peter Grimes* (Britten)

"The Sea" and "Sinbad's Ship" from *Scheherazade* (Rimsky-Korsakov)

"Play of the Waves" from *La Mer* (Debussy)

"The Hebrides Overture" (Fingal's Cave) (Mendelssohn)

"A Boat on the Ocean" from *Miroirs* (Ravel)

You can find many different musical recordings of these pieces. Ask a music teacher or librarian to help you locate some of them. What other musical pieces from the sea can you discover? Make a list of them. Share your findings and music with a group.

- If you live in one of the western states, your local fish and game division might have razorback suckers that you can view in hatcheries or refuge ponds. For example, endangered fish such as the razorback sucker live in refuge ponds at the Horsethief Canyon State Wildlife Area near Fruita in western Colorado.

- Do your part to help native fish by keeping alien fish out of streams, rivers, and lakes. Never release fish (including bait fish) into waters unless you got the fish from the same location. If you have aquarium fish but find you can no longer keep your fish, find other people to give them a new home. In some states, it is illegal to release non-native fish.

- Learn about the fish in your area, especially if you are an angler. A field guide, such as *Freshwater Fishes* by Lawrence Page and Brooks Burr (number 42 in the *Peterson Field Guide Series*) can help you identify fish you encounter.

- Razorback suckers suffer from a public relations problem. Even though the fish is endangered and its loss would inevitably be felt ecologically, it is hard to drum up support for the fish with the unappealing name. You head up a public relations firm and have just been hired to rename the razorback sucker. Study the natural history extensively and come up with three or four names that might help the image of the fish.

- With reference to the previous activity, now that you have an appealing name for the razorback sucker, plan a public relations campaign that will show the value of the fish so that people will want to join in efforts to save the species from extinction.

- Using papier-mâché, make a full-scale model of the razorback sucker.

- Organize a razorback sucker fan club. Publish a newspaper about the fish.

Chapter 7: Natural Phenomena

The following activities will help your students appreciate natural phenomena (see Figure 9.2).

Figure 9.2   Noah's Ark and rainbow art.

Rainbow Activities: Language Arts and Listening

Give out slips of paper with animals' names written on them, one for each student; there should be two slips for each animal. Have each student simultaneously make the sound of the animal whose name is written on his or her slip of paper. The object is for pairs of students to find each other, using only the animal sounds for identification. Instead of sounds, students may enjoy pantomiming actions for identification. When the activity is over, have your students line up alphabetically according to the animals' names.

Suggestions for animals:

cat	fish	wolf
dog	chipmunk	sheep
monkey	horse	rattlesnake
donkey	elephant	cow
chicken	hyena	cuckoo
lion	seal	mouse

Oral Sharing

Students' activities:

- Select one of the versions of how rainbows came to be and develop it into a story to tell.

- Are there any stories about a time in your life when you saw a rainbow? Was it special? What do you remember? Tell about it.

Writing

Students' activities:

- Write and tell your own myth explaining how the rainbow came to be in the sky.

- As a group, brainstorm which creatures did not get on the ark. Make your creatures as off-beat as possible. Then write the story of why they "missed the boat" and illustrate it.

- One story goes that when the raccoons waited to get onto the ark until after the unicorns got there, Noah's three sons slapped their hands over the raccoons' eyes and dragged them on board; that is why raccoons wear masks. Write your own version about how certain animals got their physical characteristics.

- Keep a journal of the activities you have worked on that are related to rainbows. React to each of these activities. Some possible reactions to consider: Did you learn anything new? How did it feel when you performed the activity? What do you see as possibilities for further study?

Discussion

Students' activities:

- What experiences have others had with rainbows? Tell about them. How are they alike and how are they different?

Advertising

Students' activities:

- Look through catalogs, brochures, and novelty shops to discover various marketing strategies for rainbows. Create a rainbow product of your own, develop an advertising program for it (slogan, description, or sales pitch), and test the market with your friends and families. Do you think your product would sell? Why?

Journalism

Students' activities:

- Write a class newspaper named "Rainbows." What kinds of articles would be appropriate? Remember that newspapers have different sections. Write an article about the appearance of the first rainbow as a news event; then write the story as a science fiction feature.

- Pretend that you have just discovered the pot of gold at the end of the rainbow. Call a press conference and give your story to the reporters. Remember, you must expect to answer questions starting with who, what, when, where, why, and how. Prepare an outline for your press release.

Vocabulary

Students' activities:

- Read the following sentences out loud. How are the sounds of the italicized words alike or different?

    Bow to the queen and king.

    The *bow* and arrow belong to Kim.

    The biggest *bough* of the tree was broken off.

- Look the three words up in the dictionary and write the meaning or meanings for each one.

- Where do you think the expression "We missed the boat" came from? Investigate the origin of the phrase.

Reading

Students' activities:

- Compare and contrast any two stories of how the rainbow was created.
- Use the lyrics of "Somewhere Over the Rainbow" (Harburg, 1938) or "The Unicorn" (Silverstein, n.d.) for choral reading. How will you establish the arrangement for this choral reading? How will you use your voices? What about emphasis, speed, tone, pitch, and volume?

Poetry

Students' activities:

- Collect poems related to the rainbow. Make a class book of them.
- Write an original poem about the rainbow.

Science

Students' activities:

- What colors are in a rainbow? Experiment: Place a pan of water in a beam of sunlight. Against one side of the pan, lean a small mirror. Move the mirror until you see the colors. Paint a rainbow using the colors you see.

  A rainbow in the morning
  Is the shepherd's warning;
  A rainbow at night
  Is the shepherd's delight.

- Many folk rhymes and sayings address rainbows as weather forecasters. How many can you find?

- Observe rainbows and develop some generalizations about what you see. Where is the sun (even if it is hidden by clouds) in relation to the rainbow?

- Why do you see only an arc of the rainbow instead of a full circle?

- Ask your teacher to invite a local television weatherperson to come in and speak to the class about rainbows.

- Experiment with prisms. Create and write up an experiment and see if another student can follow your directions.

- Experiment with bubbles. How many different colors can you see in the soap film? Add food coloring to a soap solution. Does the food coloring alter the colors on the surface of the bubble? Look at the bubble through colored cellophane. Do the colors in the bubble look different?

Cooking

Students' activities:

- A recipe called "Rainbow in a Cloud" calls for colored cubes of gelatin mixed into in a dish of whipped cream. Can you invent other rainbow ideas for eating? List all the ingredients and directions for making your new dish. (Maybe the prize-winning recipe could be prepared and sampled by the class.)

Art

Students' activities:

- Develop a bulletin board about the rainbow.

- Create a mural of rainbows.

- Create a stitchery collage of rainbows for a permanent school display.

- Construct a rainbow mobile and suspend drops of rain from it.

- Make puppets to use in telling the story or in singing a song about rainbows.

- Study the art and media used in picture books with rainbows. Experiment with woodcuts, linoleum cuts, and printmaking.

- Develop a class book that illustrates a myth about the rainbow. Place the finished book in the classroom or school library.

Music

Students' activities:

- Listen to recordings of rainbow songs. Create movement and dance to express the mood and words of the songs.

- Create a song about rainbows.

- Create movements to express a rainstorm, rushing water, and a rainbow.

<u>Bonus Activity</u>

- With the help of the teacher, create an activity center, which might include games you develop, class books in various stages of development, records and tapes for listening, and a collection of art and science materials, books, and other resources.

Chapter 8: Tall Tales

The tall tale is probably the most typical form of folk literature in the United States. These tales seem to express an attitude typical of our country. Characters in tall tales loom bigger and stronger than life. These exaggerations probably developed because the land, weather, geographic isolation, and natural wonders were amazing, new, awesome, and frightening to many of the pioneers. Humor, which was quite likely one of the few solaces, prevailed over the perils of the territory.

The tales weigh the delicate balance between truth and untruth in favor of untruth. Just enough truth makes good story material, and vast exaggeration imaginatively improves on the actual happenings. These stories are realistic and as convincing as possible.

The tall tale hero and heroine are always remarkable for sharp wit, physical strength, and action. They swagger, exaggerate, play tricks, and yet solve problems for mere mortals.

Folk heroes have become part of our heritage. Johnny Appleseed, Bill Pecos, Molly Brown, Paul Bunyan, Annie Christmas, Davy Crockett, Mike Find, John Henry, Joe Magarac, Alfred Bulltop Stormalong, Ichabod Crane, Casey Jones, Wild Bill Hickok, Calamity Jane, Febold Feboldson, Jim Bridger, Jebediah Smith, Finn MacCool, and Kit Carson are some of the bigger-than-life folklore population of our country.

Tall tales tell of the perplexity and watchfulness of people and their faith in themselves. We are all minor gods full of potential, hope, and humor. What comes next will be the truth, the whole truth, and everything but the truth.

These tales emerge as first-person, full-blown stories or as anecdotes (an amusing report of a single happening), and contain liberal doses of local color and circumstantial detail. They often involve bragging and boasting in rich and colorful language. The poker-faced characters swagger with a great show of reason and accuracy seasoned with lunacy.

Tall tale possibilities abound in a variety of categories, among them mining tall tales:

An Irishman was singlejacking in some tough ground one day and when he came out of the hole that night the boss said, "How'd she go today, Pat? "Begorra," said Pat, "I drilled all day on one hole and the ground's so hard that when I quit, the hole stuck out two inches."

Miner's toast: May your veins be large and your arteries flow freely. (This will insure your wealth and health.)

A miner is a liar who owns a hole in the ground (Mark Twain).

Tall Tale Activities

Students' activities:

- Weather is another wonderful topic for the tall tale. Weather is ubiquitous— it is everywhere around us. People always talk about the weather. Some samples:

    In Nebraska, farmers feed their chickens cracked ice to prevent them from laying hard-boiled eggs.

    Down by the river, it'll get so dry that the catfish will come up to the house and drink from the pump.

    In Maine, it was so hot last summer that one day, right in the middle of corn season, corn started to pop.

    There was a herd of cows grazing next to the cornfield and they saw that popcorn coming down. And cows are not very bright, of course; they thought it was snow. Every one of them idiot cows stood there and froze to death!

- Survey adults and make a list of their weather tall tales. How hot was it? How cold was it? How dry was it? How wet was it? How bad was the blizzard? Put what you collect into a "Tall Tale Weather Report" book and share it with others.

- Organize an Old-Timers tall tale contest in your community. This could be (and is) a wonderful way to honor your elders and their imaginations.

- Create tall tale stories about imaginary animals such as Wyoming's jackalope, the unicorn, etc.

- Read two or more tall tales, preferably about different tall tale heroes and heroines. Identify similarities in the tales; list the findings on the chalkboard.

- Identify in which region of the country tall tale heroes and heroines may have lived. Find clues in the tales that provide this information.

- Develop a bulletin board titled "Tall Tale Heroes, Heroines, and Animals of America." The board should have a large map of the United States (see

Figure 9.3, page 154) on which you can place names and figures of tall tale characters on the map in the approximate tall tale locale.

- Brainstorm how and why tall tales began.

- Your teacher will select a tall tale and read portions of it to the class. Notice the main character's development, physical appearance and description, evidences of great strength, seemingly impossible feats, etc. Discuss character development.

- Discuss similarities and differences in the characters of two (or more) well-known tall tales.

- Select a favorite hero or heroine from a tall tale and write one or more paragraphs describing the character; this exercise will encourage you to use your own words and phrases in writing.

- Read to locate specific parts of a tall tale that relate humorous incidents; share them with the class.

- Old-timers told many stories called "Big Windies." They often based them on someone's experience, though stretched somewhat. Ask your family if they remember any such stories.

- Write headlines using tall tale characters as they pertain to the articles in the newspaper.

- Draw a picture of your tall tale character as it would appear on the front page of a newspaper.

- Change political figures in the newspaper into tall tale characters and write a tall tale about them.

- Turn to the sports section of the newspaper; show two tall tale people confronting each other in a tennis, boxing, swimming, or bicycling event and write a story about it.

- Change several movie titles into tall tale titles.

- Write an editorial expressing the ecological values of Paul Bunyan or Johnny Appleseed's work.

- Write a lost-and-found ad about a tall tale character's belongings.

- Put an ad in the paper to sell Paul's bed. Describe his bed, the condition, and the asking price.

- Write an obituary about a tall tale hero, heroine, or animal.

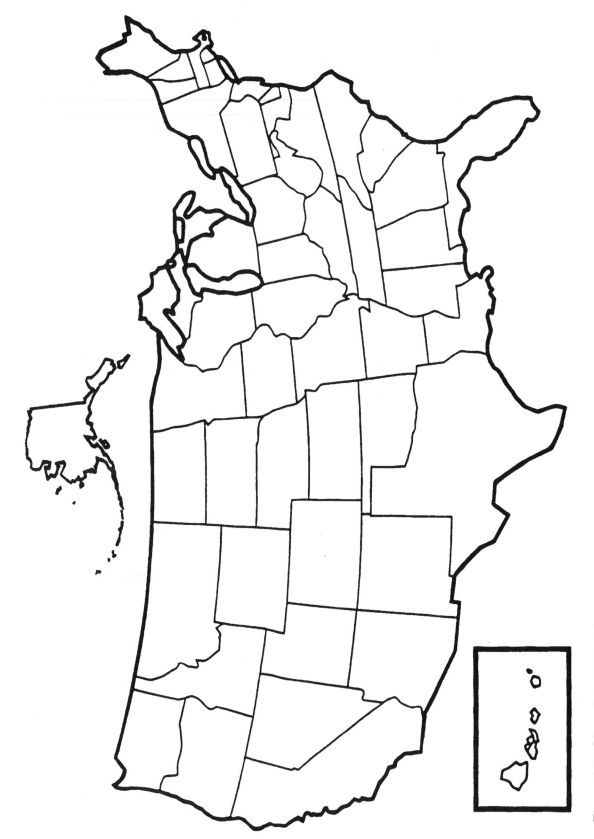

Figure 9.3   Map of the United States.

- Draw a comic strip using two characters from a tall tale.

- Write a horoscope for a tall tale character.

- Collect some of these newspaper activities and put them into a tall tale newspaper. Share this.

- Make a word search using tall tale characters.

- Create a crossword puzzle based on tall tale stories.

- Test your talents at a school-wide tall tale contest.

Additional General Activities

- Make a Mobius strip (see Figure 9.4). A Mobius strip is a one-sided surface that is constructed from a rectangular strip. Hold one end fixed and rotate the opposite end through 180 degrees. Join the ends together. If you place an X in the middle of the strip, put your pencil on it and draw a line in the middle of the strip without lifting your pencil, you will return to the X, proving that the strip has one surface. After you have made your Mobius strip, draw the life cycle of a frog so it is a never-ending cycle and starts and ends in a continuous cycle. (You could also cut out figures and paste them on your strip.)

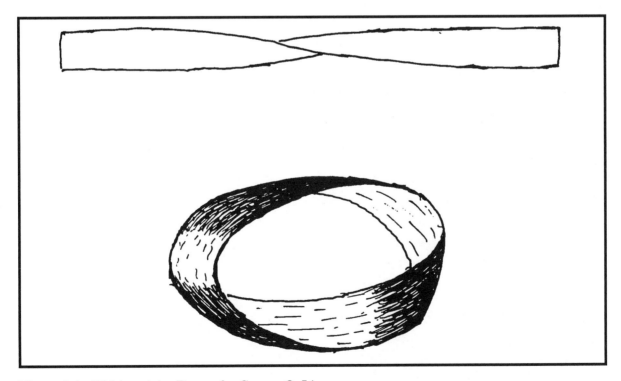

Figure 9.4   Mobius strip. Drawn by George O. Livo.

- Write a circular story about a creature and put it on a Mobius strip.

- Write a poem for a strip.

Edna St. Vincent Millay wrote a poem called "Renascence" in 1910 after she had climbed Mount Battie in Camden Hills (see Figure 9.5). She was 15 years old when she wrote it. This poem appears on a bronze marker at the top of the mountain:

> All I could see from where I stood
>
> Was three long mountains and a wood,
>
> I turned and looked another way
>
> And saw three islands in a bay.
>
> So with my eyes I traced the line
>
> Of the horizons thin and fine.
>
> Straight around till I was come
>
> Back to where I started from,
>
> And all I saw from where I stood
>
> Was three long mountains and a wood.

Figure 9.5   Plaque illustrating Edna St. Vincent Millay's poem, "Renascence." Photo by Norma J. Livo.

- Draw a picture based on Millay's circular poem.

- Cut out cartoon characters from the comic section of your newspaper. Write a story about them

  in the forest;

  in the desert;

  in the high mountains;

  in a corn field; or

  on a lake shore.

Illustrate your story with these cartoon characters.

- Write the story of "Peter and the Wolf" in Readers' Theatre format. Share it with others.

- Rewrite "Peter and the Wolf" with the wolf as the hero or the wolf as the duck character.

- Pick any creature and write a story about it and set it to music. Dance or act your story with friends.

- Listen to a record of frogs. (Better yet, in the spring go to a local lake where frogs live and tape these sounds yourself.) Play the frog sounds and draw pictures while listening to it. Share your picture with others.

- Play "The Moldau" by Bedrich Smetana. This is one of the few examples in musical literature in which the flowing of water inspired a composer to represent the river as a living being. It is the musical story of two tiny streams that become a great river with a character of its own. The river represents the growth and passing of human existence. While you listen to the music, draw pictures of ideas and thoughts you hear in the music. Share your pictures with others.

- Go on an oral history collection project to tape people's images from their lives in the landscapes of their youth. Tape these stories and anecdotes from their pasts. What did they do as kids? What places have changed since they were young? A good person to interview might be a caretaker of one of the Nature Conservancy projects. (The Nature Conservancy is a nonprofit organization involved in environmental issues. Some people say these projects should develop good records about these special landscapes. They also say that we need to learn more from the people who have lived in the areas represented. It is essential to preserve these memories before frenzied growth takes over the land.)

- It has been said that art is the recorder of truth. From the story of the magic flute given by the elk, what would it take to make yourself a flute from natural material? Experiment with your homemade flute. Does the length and fingering spaces of flutes make any difference?

- Collect a file of newspaper articles about the environment. Can you classify them into a variety of categories?

- Create riddles that describe particular plants, animals or people from a story. Share these riddles with others.

- Dress up as a plant or animal from a story and hold a party that everyone attends in costume.

- Turn a story into a puppet show or play to perform.

- Create a mural or collage exploring a story and the lessons it teaches.

- Find and share a story from your family background. Where did your family come from in "the old country?"

- There are many ways to tell a story. You can sing a story, write a story, dance a story, act out a story, paint a story or sew a storytelling cloth. A storytelling cloth can be made from appliqués sewed to a larger solid-colored cloth. Embroidery (an easy stitch) fills in the details, such as feathers on a bird.

- Play with language in as many ways as you can. For instance, read the following anonymous poem:

> As wet as a fish—as dry as a bone;
>
> As live as a bird—as dead as a stone;
>
> As plump as a partridge—as poor as a rat;
>
> As strong as a horse—as weak as a cat;
>
> As hard as a flint—as soft as a mole;
>
> As white as a lily—as black as a coal;
>
> As plain as a staff—as rough as a bear;
>
> As light as a drum—as free as the air;
>
> As heavy as lead—as light as a feather;
>
> As steady as time—uncertain as weather;
>
> As hot as an oven—as cold as a frog;
>
> As gay as a lark—as sick as a dog;
>
> As savage as tigers—as mild as a dove;
>
> As stiff as a poker—as limp as a glove;

As blind as a bat—as deaf as a post;

As cool as a cucumber—as warm as toast;

As flat as a flounder—as round as a ball;

As blunt as a hammer—as sharp as an awl;

As brittle as glass—as tough as gristle;

As neat as a pin—as clean as a whistle;

As red as a rose—as square as a box,

As bold as a thief—as sly as a fox.

Many comparisons older than time!

Perhaps you can think of some others that rhyme.

Did this poem trigger ideas for something you could write? Add to it if you can. Form small groups to brainstorm ideas. List your ideas and put them on a bulletin board. Good luck!

Petroglyphs and Petrographs

Petroglyphs are carved, pecked, or scratched into rocks, while petrographs are painted directly on the rock. Before words, letters, or alphabets, there was rock art—writing with pictures—communicating with images. These images were made on available smooth rock surfaces, boulders, rock ledges, canyon walls, cliffs, and caves. They are found in Australia, France, Scandinavia, the United States (including Hawaii and Alaska), the Caribbean, and Canada. These images were important stories for the people.

They were made thousands of years ago in many cases. For instance, the Sami (Laplanders) of Scandinavian petroglyphs that were discovered in the summer of 1984 at Umea, numbered roughly 60 carvings of elk, reindeer, people, boats, and hunting scenes. The petroglyphs were found on rocks that formed an island in a wide river. They were created by Stone Age people who inhabited this area. (See Figure 9.6, page 160.)

Since everything in nature was considered alive and sacred, these works of rock art are records of truths that were worshipped in sacred places. They illustrated rites and were maps for travelers. Usually religious leaders created the rock art as part of their rituals.

In general, rock art expressed the inner, unconscious world of dreams, visions, and feelings. In the rock carvings and paintings of the world, there are monsters, warriors, and flute players as well as animals, birds, reptiles, and symbols of natural phenomena such as lightening.

Students' Activities

- Develop a design and use it to make borders on paper. Use this as note/writing paper, gift wrap, place mats, or pages in a book.

- Write a story about one of the pictured petroglyphs (see Figures 9.6–9.10). Who are the characters, what are the events pictured? What happened?

- Share this story with others.

- Carve designs into clay that will harden, wood, or plaster. Put a piece of paper or cloth over this surface, then rub a crayon over it to capture the design. These are called rubbings.

- What designs can you create to illustrate important places, creatures, plants, and people in your life?

- Sami (Laplanders) rock art depicts boats and reindeer predominately. Why is this?

- Study the Native American and Sami rock carvings. How are they alike and how are they different? Why?

- Locate on a map of the world where various examples of rock art can be found.

The following photographs show petroglyphs (see Figures 9.6 –9.10). Find the animals (real and fictional) and study them.

Figure 9.6   Petroglyph Samples from Umea, Sweden, and Northern Finland.

Figure 9.7   Petroglyphs.

Figure 9.8   Petroglyphs.

Figure 9.9   Petroglyphs.

Figure 9.10   Petroglyphs.

Resources

RESOURCE INFORMATION

When you need to find out more information about animals and what is being done to preserve and protect them, contact the following groups:

The Conservation Foundation
1717 Massachusetts Avenue, NW
Washington, DC 20036

National Audubon Society
950 Third Avenue
New York, NY 10022

Council on Economic Priorities
456 Greenwich Street
New York, NY 10013

National Parks and Conservation
    Association
1701 18th Street, NW
Washington, DC 20009

Defenders of Wildlife
2000 N Street, NW
Washington, DC 20036

National Wildlife Federation
1400 16th Street, NW
Washington, DC 20036

Environmental Action, Inc.
1346 Connecticut Avenue, NW
Room 731
Washington, DC 20036

National Resources Council of
    America
1025 Connecticut Avenue, NW
Suite 911
Washington, DC 20036

Environmental Defense Fund, Inc.
162 Old Town Road
East Setauket, NY 11733

Natural Resources Defense Council
40 West 20th Street
New York, NY 10011

Friends of the Earth
529 Commercial Street
San Francisco, CA 94111

The Nature Conservancy
1815 North Lynn Street
Arlington, VA 22209

Greenpeace USA
1436 U Street
Washington, DC 20009

Scientists' Institute for Public
    Information
438 North Skinker
St. Louis, MO 63130

League of Women Voters of the U.S.
1730 M Street, NW
Washington, DC 20036

Sierra Club
Public Affairs Department
730 Polk Street
San Francisco, CA 94109

Wildlife Management Institute
709 Wire Building
Washington, DC 20005

The Wilderness Society
900 17th Street, NW
Washington, DC 20006

Wilderness Watch
P.O. Box 3184
Green Bay, WI 54303

World Wildlife Fund/Conservation
    Foundation
1250 24th Street, NW
Suite 400
Washington, DC 20037

Bibliography

Baylor, Byrd. *Coyote Cry.* Illustrated by Symeon Shimin. New York: Lothrop, Lee & Shepard, 1972.

Betancourt, Jeanne. *Ten True Animal Rescues.* New York: Scholastic, 1998.

Bierhorst, John. *Doctor Coyote.* Illustrated by Wendy Watson. New York: Macmillan, 1987.

Botkin, B. A., ed. *A Treasury of American Folklore.* New York: Crown, 1944.

Bradman, Tony, and Margaret Chamberlain. *Who's Afraid of the Big Bad Wolf?* New York: Macmillan/Alladin, 1989.

Coffin, Tristram Potter, and Henning Cohen, eds. *Folklore from the Working Folk of America.* New York: Anchor Press, 1973.

Colorado Wildlife. "The Colorado Chronicles." Vol. 5. Frederick, Colo.: Jende-Hagan Bookcorp, 1983.

Delaney, A. *The Gunnywolf.* New York: Harper & Row, 1988.

Dettmer, Mary Lou. *Little Red Riding Hood.* Morton Grove, Ill.: Whitman, 1971.

Diendorfer, Robert G. *America's 101 Most High Falutin', Big Talkin', Knee Slappin' Gollywhoppers and Tall Tales: The Best of the Burlington Liars Club.* New York: Workman, 1980.

Elting, Mary. *The Answer Book About Animals.* Illustrated by Rowan Barnes-Murphy. New York: Grosset & Dunlap, 1984.

Emrich, Duncan. *The Hodgepodge Book.* New York: Four Winds Press, 1972.

Fredericks, Anthony. *Exploring the Oceans.* Illustrated by Shawn Shea. Golden, Colo.: Fulcrum Publishing, 1998.

Gardner, Howard. *Frames of Mind.* New York: Basic Books. 1993.

———. *The Unschooled Mind: How Children Think and How Schools Should Teach.* New York: Basic Books, 1991.

———. *Multiple Intelligences: The Theory in Practice.* New York: Basic Books, 1993.

———. *Leading Minds: An Anatomy of Leadership.* New York: Basic Books, 1995.

———. *Extraordinary Minds: Portraits of Exceptional Individuals and an Examination of Our Extraordinariness.* New York: Basic Books, 1997.

Gardner, Howard, M. Kornhaber, and W. Wake. *Intelligence: Multiple Perspectives.* Fort Worth, Tex.: Harcourt Brace, 1996.

Gay, Michel. *The Christmas Wolf.* New York: Greenwillow, 1980.

George, Jean Craighead. *Julie of the Wolves.* Illustrated by Sal Catalano. New York: HarperCollins, 1972.

———. *The Moon of the Gray Wolves.* Illustrated by Sal Catalano. New York: HarperCollins, 1991.

———. *The Wounded Wolf.* Illustrated by John Schoenherr. New York: Harper & Row, 1978.

Goble, Paul. *Dream Wolf.* New York: Bradbury, 1990.

Grimm, Jacob, and Wilhelm Grimm. "The Wolf and the Seven Little Kids," "The Wolf and the Fox," "The Wolf and the Man," "Gossip Wolf and the Fox," and "Little Red Riding Hood." In *Grimm's Complete Fairy Tales.* New York: Nelson Doubleday, n.d.

———. *Little Red Riding Hood.* Illustrated by Bernadette. New York: Scholastic, 1971.

Grinnell, George Bird. *By Cheyenne Campfires.* Lincoln, Nebr.: University of Nebraska Press, 1971.

Harper, Wilhelmina. *The Gunniwolf.* Illustrated by William Wiesner. New York: Dutton, 1967.

Hillerman, Tony. *Coyote Waits.* New York: Harper & Row, 1990.

Hyman, Trina Schart. *Little Red Riding Hood.* New York: Holiday House, 1983.

Lauber, Patricia. *Great Whales.* Illustrated by Pieter Folkens. New York: Henry Holt, 1991.

Ling, Mary. *Eyewitness Juniors: Amazing Wolves, Dogs, and Foxes.* Photographs by Jerry Young. New York: Knopf, 1991.

Livo, Norma J., and George O. Livo. *The Enchanted Wood and Other Tales from Finland.* Englewood, Colo.: Libraries Unlimited, 1999.

Livo, Norma J., and Sandra A. Rietz. *Storytelling Process and Practice.* Littleton, Colo.: Libraries Unlimited, 1986.

———. *Storytelling Activities.* Littleton, Colo.: Libraries Unlimited, 1987.

Livo, Lauren J., Glenn McGlathery, and Norma J. Livo. *Of Bugs and Beasts.* Englewood, Colo.: Teacher Ideas Press, 1995.

Lopez, Barry Holstun. *Of Wolves and Men.* New York: Scribner's, 1978.

Malterre, Elona. *The Last Wolf of Ireland.* New York: Clarion, 1990.

McGlathery, Glenn, and Norma J. Livo. *Who's Endangered on Noah's Ark?* Englewood, Colo.: Teacher Ideas Press, 1992.

McPhail, David. *A Wolf Story.* New York: Scribner's, 1981.

Mora, Francisco X. *The Coyote Rings the Wrong Bell.* Chicago, Ill.: Children's Press, 1991.

Morris, Ann. *The Little Red Riding Hood Rebus Book.* Illustrated by Ljiljana Rylands. New York: Orchard Books, 1987.

Mowat, Farley. *Never Cry Wolf.* New York: Franklin Watts, 1963.

Myers, Walter Dean. *The Story of the Three Kingdoms.* Illustrated by Ashley Bryan. New York: HarperCollins, 1995.

Norman, Howard. "Coyote and Fox." *Northern Tales.* New York: Pantheon, 1990.

Patent, Dorothy Hinshaw. *All About Whales.* New York: Holiday House, 1987.

———. *Gray Wolf, Red Wolf.* Photographs by William Munoz. New York: Clarion, 1990.

———. *Humpback Whales.* Photography by Mark J. Ferrari and Deborah A. Glockner-Ferrari. New York: Holiday House, 1989.

———. *Killer Whales.* Photographs by John K. B. Ford. New York: Holiday House, 1993.

———. *Whales, Giants of the Deep.* New York: Holiday House, 1984.

Perrault, Charles. *Little Red Riding Hood.* Illustrated by Sarah Moon. Mankato, Minn.: Creative Education, 1983.

Prokofiev, Serge. *Peter and the Wolf.* Illustrated by Warren Chappell. New York: Alfred A. Knopf, 1940.

Roessel, Robert A., Jr., and Dillon Platero. *Coyote Stories of the Navajo People.* Phoenix, Ariz.: Navajo Curriculum Center Press, 1974.

Root, Phyllis. *Coyote and the Magic Words.* Illustrated by Sandra Speidel. New York: Lothrop, Lee & Shepard, 1993.

Sara. *The Rabbit, the Fox, and the Wolf.* New York: Orchard Books, 1991.

Sattler, Helen Roney. *Whales.* Illustrated by Jean Day Zallinger. New York: Lothrop, Lee & Shepard, 1987.

Scally, Kevin. *The Story of Little Red Riding Hood.* New York: Grosset & Dunlap, 1984.

Schwartz, Alvin. *Whoppers: Tall Tales and Other Lies.* New York: J. B. Lippincott, 1975.

Sciezka, Jon. *The True Story of the Three Little Pigs.* Illustrated by Lane Smith. New York: Viking Kestrel, 1989.

Shirley, Gaayle C. *Four-Legged Legends of Colorado.* Helena, Mont.: Falcon, 1994.

Simon, Tony, ed. *Ripsnorters and Ribticklers: Tall Tales from United States Folklore.* New York: Scholastic, 1958.

Stevens, Janet. *Coyote Steals the Blanket.* New York: Holiday House, 1993.

Stone, George. *A Legend of Wolf Song.* New York: Grosset & Dunlap, 1975.

Thurber, James. "The Little Girl and the Wolf." In *Fables of Our Times.* New York: Harper & Row, 1940.

Yolen, Jane. "Wolf Child" and "Happy Dens; or, A Day in the Old Wolves' Home." In *The Faery Flag.* New York: Orchard Books, 1989.

Index

More Science Class Fun

from *Teacher Ideas Press*

CLOSE ENCOUNTERS WITH DEADLY DANGERS: Riveting Reads and Classroom Ideas
Kendall Haven

Predators and prey of the animal kingdom hunt, fight, and survive in these spine-tingling accounts that will enthrall your students. Fifteen action-packed tales are filled with accurate scientific information on many of the world's ecosystems and their inhabitants, including lions, anacondas, and sharks. Suggestions for activities and research follow each story. **Grades 4–8**.
xv, 149p. 6x9 paper ISBN 1-56308-653-0

SOARING THROUGH THE UNIVERSE: Astronomy Through Children's Literature
Joanne C. Letwinch

Get students to reach for the stars—Teach the basics of astronomical and space science using traditional folktales and children's literature. Chapters on the moon, sun, planets, stars, and flight offer reproducible activities and project ideas that combine stories and facts with multiple subject areas. Resources for further out-of-this-world research are included. **Grades 3–6**.
xvi, 191p. 8½x11 paper ISBN 1-56308-560-7

A SENSE OF PLACE: Teaching Children about the Environment with Picture Books
Daniel A. Kriesberg

Introduce young learners to the wonders of nature by celebrating our own backyards. Focusing on the five senses, simple activities and quality fiction and nonfiction are used to build connections between students and the land around them. **Grades K–6**.
xxvii, 145p. 8½x11 paper ISBN 1-56308-565-8

EXPLORING THE ENVIRONMENT THROUGH CHILDREN'S LITERATURE
An Integrated Approach
Carol M. Butzow and John W. Butzow

Teach children about nature with quality literature and hands-on activities that support environmental themes and principles. Contemporary and classic children's books provide a springboard for activities that span the curriculum. Puzzles, word searches, suggestions for computer usage, and library connections round out 15 chapters of fun.
Grades K–4 (adaptable to higher levels).
xii, 163p. 8½x11 paper ISBN 1-56308-650-6

TEACHER'S WEATHER SOURCEBOOK: Information, Ideas, and Activities
Tom Konvicka

Answer students weather-related questions and plan stimulating lessons on topics such as global warming, tornadoes, air pollution, and acid deposition.
Grades 4–8.
xvi, 321p. 8½x11 paper ISBN 1-56308-488-0

For a free catalog or to place an order, please contact: Teacher Ideas Press/Libraries Unlimited.
• Phone: 1-800-237-6124
• Fax: 303-220-8843
• E-mail: lu-books@lu.com
• Mail to: Dept. B014 • P.O. Box 6633
       Englewood, CO 80155-6633